Defoe Abbott Marx Hardy Melville Montaigne Machiavelli Haggard Chesterton Cooper Emerson Joyce Austen Hugo Eliot Grimm

Stoker Christie Carroll Maupassant Byron Engels Schiller Molière

Wilde Garnett Fitzgerald Einstein Hawthorne Smith Kafka

Goethe Cotton Dostoyevsky Doyle Hall Willis

Baum Henry Kipling Nietzsche Balzac

Leslie Dumas Flaubert Turgenev Crane

Stockton Vatsyayana Verne

Burroughs Vinci

Curtis Tocqueville Gogol Busch

Homer Widger Tolstoy Whitman

Darwin Thoreau Twain Scott Plato Harte

Potter Freud Zola Lawrence Dickens Burton Hesse

Kant Jowett Stevenson

Andersen Voltaire Cervantes

London Descartes Cooke

Poe Aristotle Wells

Hale James Hastings Irving

Bunner Shakespeare

Richter Chambers da Shaw Benedict Alcott

Doré Dante Chekhov Wodehouse Pushkin

Swift Newton

# tredition

tredition was established in 2006 by Sandra Latusseck and Soenke Schulz. Based in Hamburg, Germany, tredition offers publishing solutions to authors and publishing houses, combined with world-wide distribution of printed and digital book content. tredition is uniquely positioned to enable authors and publishing houses to create books on their own terms and without conventional manufacturing risks.

For more information please visit: www.tredition.com

TREDITION CLASSICS

This book is part of the TREDITION CLASSICS series. The creators of this series are united by passion for literature and driven by the intention of making all public domain books available in printed format again - worldwide. Most TREDITION CLASSICS titles have been out of print and off the bookstore shelves for decades. At tredition we believe that a great book never goes out of style and that its value is eternal. Several mostly non-profit literature projects provide content to tredition. To support their good work, tredition donates a portion of the proceeds from each sold copy. As a reader of a TREDITION CLASSICS book, you support our mission to save many of the amazing works of world literature from oblivion. See all available books at www.tredition.com.

Project Gutenberg

The content for this book has been graciously provided by Project Gutenberg. Project Gutenberg is a non-profit organization founded by Michael Hart in 1971 at the University of Illinois. The mission of Project Gutenberg is simple: To encourage the creation and distribution of eBooks. Project Gutenberg is the first and largest collection of public domain eBooks.

Journal of the Third Voyage for the Discovery of a North-West Passage

William Edward, Sir Parry

Imprint

This book is part of TREDITION CLASSICS

Author: William Edward, Sir Parry
Cover design: Buchgut, Berlin – Germany

Publisher: tredition GmbH, Hamburg - Germany
ISBN: 978-3-8472-1675-9

www.tredition.com
www.tredition.de

JOURNAL
OF THE
THIRD VOYAGE
FOR THE DISCOVERY OF A
NORTH-WEST PASSAGE.

by
CAPT. W. E. PARRY, R.N., F.R.S.,
and commander of the expedition.

CASSELL & COMPANY, Limited:
LONDON, PARIS, NEW YORK & MELBOURNE.
1889.

p. 5INTRODUCTION.

William Edward Parry, the son of a physician, was born at Bath in December, 1790. At the age of thirteen he was entered as a first-class volunteer on board the flag-ship of the Channel fleet, and after seven years' service and careful study of his profession he obtained a commission in 1810 as lieutenant in the navy. He was then at once, aged twenty, sent to the Arctic seas, where he was during two or three years in command of a ship for protection of the British whale fisheries and for revision of the admiralty charts. In 1813 he was recalled from that service and sent on blockade service to the North American station, where he remained about four years, and occupied his leisure in writing a book on "Nautical Astronomy by Night," which he published upon his return to England in 1817.

At that time the search for a North-West Passage to Eastern Asia had been suspended for more than half a century. No expedition had been sent p. 6out since 1746. But after Lieutenant Parry's return from the North American station, an expedition was prepared under Sir John Ross in the *Isabella*, which sailed in April, 1818, accompanied by the *Alexander*, to the command of which Parry was appointed, Sir John Ross being chief of the expedition. They went by Davis's Straits to Lancaster Sound, where Sir John Ross gave up hope of success and turned back; though Lieutenant Parry would have gone on. Next year Parry was entrusted with an expedition of his own, which set out in May, 1819, and reached Lancaster Sound in July, discovered Prince Regent's Inlet, and Barrow Straits, named after Sir John Barrow, Secretary to the Admiralty, who was active promoter of these expeditions. Parry wintered among the ice and returned next year, having pushed Arctic discovery by thirty degrees of longitude farther than any who had gone before. That was Parry's first voyage, from which he returned to be received with triumph by his countrymen. He was advanced to the rank of Commander in November, 1820, and made a Fellow of the Royal Society. He had shown in what direction to proceed with further search, and at the age of thirty p. 7had established for himself a place of lasting honour in the history of English navigation.

Commander Parry was sent on a second expedition in 1821, from which he returned in 1823. He was to explore the Fox Channel, for the purpose of ascertaining whether it was connected with the Arctic Sea of his first voyage. This voyage had no important results; and in 1824 Parry started again on the third voyage, of which this volume contains his Journal. In 1827 he sailed again in the *Hecla*, but found himself sledging over ice that floated southward as fast as he travelled forward on it northward. He returned then to the work ashore, as a hydrographer, for which his thorough knowledge of navigation marked him out. Desire for a more active life caused him to spend four or five years in Australia (from 1829 to 1834) as Commissioner to the Agricultural Company of Australia. He was knighted, and became in 1852 a Rear-Admiral. Sir Edward Parry was Lieutenant-Governor of Greenwich Hospital at the time of his death, in July, 1855.

H. M.

p. 9THIRD VOYAGE FOR THE DISCOVERY OF A NORTH-WEST PASSAGE.

INTRODUCTION.

Notwithstanding the want of success of the late Expedition to the Polar Seas, it was resolved to make another attempt to effect a passage by sea, between the Atlantic and Pacific Oceans. The chief attentions in the equipment of the present expedition consisted in the placing of Sylvester's warming stove in the very bottom of the ship's hold, in substituting a small quantity of salt beef for a part of the pork, and in furnishing a much larger supply of newly corned beef. Preserved carrots and parsnips, salmon, cream, pickles of onions, beetroot, cabbage, and, to make the most of our stowage, split pease instead of whole ones, were supplied. A small quantity of beef pemmican, made by pounding the meat with a certain portion of fat, as described by Captain Franklin, was also furnished.

To the officers, seamen, and marines my best acknowledgments are once more due, for the zealous support I have at all times received from them in the course of this service; and I am happy to repeat my conviction that, had it depended on their conduct and exertion, our most sanguine expectations would, long ere this, have been crowned with complete success.

p. 10CHAPTER I.

Passage to the Whale-fish Islands, and Removal of Stores from the Transport—Enter the Ice in Baffin's Bay—Difficulties of Penetrating to the Westward—Quit the Ice in Baffin's Bay—Remarks on the Obstructions encountered by the Ships, and on the Severity of the Season.

The equipment of the *Hecla* and *Fury*, and the loading of the *William Harris* transport, being completed, we began to move down the river from Deptford on the 8th of May, 1824, and on the 10th, by the assistance of the steamboat, the three ships had reached Northfleet, where they received their powder and their ordnance stores. Two days were here employed in fixing, under the superintendence of Mr. Barlow and Lieutenant Foster, the plate, invented by the former gentleman, for correcting the deviation of the compass produced by the attraction of the ship's iron; and the continuance of strong easterly winds prevented our getting to the Nore till the 16th. During our stay at Northfleet the ships were visited by Viscount Melville, and the other Lords Commissioners of the Admiralty, who were pleased to approve of our general equipment and arrangements.

During our passage across the Atlantic in June, and afterwards on our way up Davis's Strait, we threw overboard daily a strong copper cylinder, containing the usual papers, giving an account of our situation. We also took every opportunity afforded by light winds, to try the temperature of the sea at different depths, as compared with that at the surface.

I now determined, as the quickest and most secure mode of clearing the transport, to anchor at the Whale-fish Islands, rather than incur the risk of hampering and p. 11damaging her among the ice. Fresh gales and thick weather, however, prevented our doing so till the 26th, when we anchored at eight A.M., in seventeen fathoms, mooring the ships by hawsers to the rocks, and then immediately commenced our work. In the meantime the observatory and instruments were landed on a small island, called by the Danes Boat Island, where Lieutenant Foster and myself carried on the magnetic and other observations during the stay of the Expedition at this anchorage, of which a survey was also made.

Early on the morning of the 3rd of July, the whole of our stores being removed, and Lieutenant Pritchard having received his orders, together with our despatches and letters for England, the *William Harris* weighed with a light wind from the northward, and was towed out to sea by our boats. The day proving calm, we employed it in swinging the *Hecla*, in order to obtain the amount of the deviation of the magnetic needle, and to fix afresh the iron plate for correcting it. On the following morning, the wind being southerly, the pilots came on board, and the *Hecla* weighed to run through the north passage; in doing which she grounded on a rock lying directly in the channel, and having only thirteen feet upon it at low water, which our sounding boats had missed, and of which the pilot was ignorant. The tide being that of ebb we were unable to heave the ship off immediately, and at low water she had sewed three feet forward. It was not till half-past one P.M., that she floated, when it became necessary to drop her down between the rock and the shore with hawsers; after which we made sail, and being soon after joined by the *Fury*, which came out by the other channel, we stood round the islands to the northwards. This rock was not p. 12the only one found by our boats which may prove dangerous to ships going in and out of this harbour, and with which our pilots were unacquainted. Another was discovered by Mr. Head, about one-third of the distance across from Kron Prins Island to the opposite shore of the S.E. entrance, and has not more than eighteen feet water on it at low tide; it lies very much in the way of ships coming in at that channel, which is the most commonly used. The latitude of the island, on which the observations were made, called by the Danes Boat Island, is 740 28' 15"; its longitude by our chronometers, 530 12' 56"; the dip of the magnetic needle, 820 53' 66"; and the variation, 700 23' 57" westerly. The time of high water, at new moon, on the 26th of June, was a quarter-past eight, the highest tides being the third and fourth after the conjunction, and the perpendicular rise seven feet and a half.

The ships standing in towards Lively on the afternoon of the 5th, Lieutenant Graah very kindly came off to the *Fury*, which happened to be the nearest in shore, for the purpose of taking leave of us. On his quitting the ship a salute of ten guns was fired at Lievely, which we returned with an equal number; and I sent to Lieutenant Graah, by a canoe that came on board the *Hecla*, an account of the situation of the rocks we had discovered. Light northerly winds, together with the dull sailing of our now deeply laden ships, prevented our making much progress for several days, and kept us in the neighbourhood of numerous icebergs, which it is dangerous to approach when there is any swell. We counted from the deck, at one time, no less than one hundred and three of these immense bodies, some of them from one to two hundred feet in height above the sea; and it was necessary, p. 13in one or two instances, to tow the ships clear of them with the boats. We had occasion, about this time, to remark the more than usual frequency of fogs with a northerly wind, a circumstance from which the whalers are accustomed to augur a considerable extent of open water in that direction.

The ice soon beginning to close around us, our progress became so slow that, on the 17th, we saw a ship at the margin of the "pack," and two more on the following day. We supposed these to be whalers, which, after trying to cross the ice to the northward, had returned to make the attempt in the present latitude; a supposition which our subsequent difficulties served to strengthen. From this time, indeed, the obstructions from the quantity, magnitude, and closeness of the ice, were such as to keep our people almost constantly employed in heaving, warping, or sawing through it; and yet with so little success that, at the close of the month of July, we had only penetrated seventy miles to the westward, or to the longitude of about 620 10'. Here, while closely beset, on the 1st of August, we encountered a hard gale from the south-east, which pressing the ice together in every direction, by mass overlaying mass for hours together, the *Hecla* received several very awkward "nips," and was once fairly laid on her broadside by a strain which must inevitably have crushed a vessel of ordinary strength. In such cases, the ice is forced under a ship's bottom on one side, and on the other up her side, both powers thus acting in such a manner as to bring her on her "beam-ends." This is, in fact, the most favourable manner in which a ship can receive the pressure, and would perhaps only occur with ice comparatively not very heavy, though sufficiently so, it is said, to have run completely over a p. 14ship in some extreme and fatal cases. With ice of still more formidable dimensions a vessel would probably, by an equal degree of pressure, be absolutely crushed, in consequence of the increased difficulty of sinking it on one side, and causing it to rise on the other.

Sept. 9th.—I shall doubtless be readily excused for not having entered in this journal a detailed narrative of the obstacles we met with, and of the unwearied exertions of the officers and men to overcome them, during the tedious eight weeks employed in crossing this barrier. I have avoided this detail because, while it might appear an endeavour to magnify ordinary difficulties, which it is our business to overcome rather than to discuss, I am convinced that no description of mine, nor even the minute formality of the log-book, could convey an adequate idea of the truth. The strain we constantly had occasion to heave on the hawsers, as springs to force the ships through the ice, was such as perhaps no ships ever before attempted; and by means of Phillips's invaluable capstan, we often separated floes of such magnitude as must otherwise have baffled every effort. In doing this, it was next to impossible to avoid exposing the men to very great risk from the frequent breaking of the hawsers. On one occasion, three of the *Hecla's* seamen were knocked down as instantaneously as by a gunshot by the sudden flying-out of an anchor; and a marine of the *Fury* suffered in a similar manner when working at the capstan; but, providentially, they all escaped with severe contusions. A more serious accident occurred in the breaking of the spindle of the *Fury's* windlass, depriving her of the use of the windlass-end during the rest of the season.

The constant besetment of the ships, and our daily p. 15observations for latitude and longitude, afforded a favourable opportunity for ascertaining precisely the set of any currents by which the whole body of ice might be actuated. By attending very carefully to all the circumstances, it was evident that a daily set to the southward obtained, when the wind was northerly, differing in amount from two or three to eight or ten miles per day, according to the strength of the breeze; but a northerly current was equally apparent, and fully to the same amount, whenever the wind blew from the southward. A circumstance more remarkable than these, however, forced itself strongly upon my notice at this time, which was, that a *westerly* set was very frequently apparent, even against a fresh breeze blowing from that quarter. I mention the circumstance in this place, because I may hereafter have to offer a remark or two on this fact in connection with some others of a similar nature noticed elsewhere.

With respect to the dimensions of the ice through which we had now scrambled our way, principally by warping and towing a distance of between three and four hundred miles, I remarked that it for the most part increased, as well in the thickness as the extent of the floes, as we advanced westward about the parallel of 710. During our subsequent progress to the north, we also met with some of enormous dimensions, several of the floes, to which we applied our hawsers and the power of the improved capstan, being at their margin more than twenty feet above the level of the sea, and over some of these we could not see from the mast-head. Upon the whole, however, the magnitude of the ice became somewhat less towards the north-west; and within thirty miles of that margin the masses were comparatively p. 16small, and their thickness much diminished. Bergs were in sight during the whole passage; but they were more numerous towards the middle of the "pack," and rather the most so to the southward.

CHAPTER II.

Enter Sir James Lancaster's Sound—Land at Cape Warrender—Meet with young ice—Ships beset and carried near the shore—Driven back to Navy-board Inlet—Run to the westward, and enter Prince Regent's Inlet—Arrival at Port Bowen.

All our past obstacles were in a moment forgotten when we once more saw an open sea before us; but it must be confessed that it was not so easy to forget that the middle of September was already near at hand, without having brought us even to the entrance of Sir James Lancaster's Sound. That not a moment might be lost, however, in pushing to the westward, a press of canvas was crowded, and being happily favoured with an easterly breeze, on the morning of the 10th of September we caught a glimpse of the high bold land on the north side of the magnificent inlet up which our course was once more to be directed. From the time of our leaving the main body of ice we met with none of any kind, and the entrance to the Sound was, as usual, entirely free from it, except here and there a berg, floating about in that solitary grandeur of which these enormous masses, when occurring in the midst of an extensive sea, are calculated to convey so sublime an idea.

On the morning of the 11th, the ships being taken a-back with a fresh westerly breeze when near Cape Warrender, I landed in a small bay close to the westward p. 17of it, accompanied by several of the officers, in order to examine the country, and to make the necessary observations.

On the morning of the 12th we were once more favoured with a breeze from the eastward, but so light and unsteady that our progress was vexatiously slow; and on the 13th, when within seven leagues of Cape York, we had the mortification to perceive the sea ahead of us covered with young ice, the thermometer having for two days past ranged only from 180 to 200. On reaching it we had, as usual, recourse to "sallying," breaking it with boats ahead, and various other expedients, all alike ineffectual without a fresh and free breeze furnishing a constant impetus; so that, after seven or eight hours of unsuccessful labour in this way, we were obliged to remain as we were, fairly and immovably beset.

It now appeared high time to determine as to the propriety of still continuing our efforts to push to the westward or of returning to England, according to my instructions on that head under particular circumstances. As the crossing of the ice in Baffin's Bay had of itself unexpectedly occupied nearly the whole of one season, it could not, of course, be considered that the attempt to penetrate to the westward in the manner directed by their lordships had as yet been made, nor could it, indeed, be made during the present year. I could not, therefore, have a moment's hesitation as to the propriety of pushing on as far as the present season would permit, and then giving a fair trial during the whole of the next summer to the route I was directed by my instructions to pursue. In order, however, to confirm my own opinion on this subject, I requested to be furnished with that of Captain Hoppner; and finding that his views entirely agreed with p. 18my own, I resolved still to pursue our object by all the means in our power.

The next breeze sprang up from the westward, drawing also from the southward at times, out of Prince Regent's Inlet, and for three days we were struggling with the young ice to little or no purpose, now and then gaining half a mile of ground to windward in a little "hole" of open water, then losing as much by the necessity of bearing up or wearing (for the ice was too strong to allow us to tack), sallying from morning to night with all hands, and with the watch at night, two boats constantly under the bows; and, after all, rather losing ground than otherwise, while the young ice was every hour increasing in thickness.

On the 17th, when we had driven back rather to the eastward of Admiralty Inlet, an easterly breeze again enabled us to make some progress. The sea was now for the most part covered with young ice, which had become so thick as to look white throughout its whole extent. The holes of water could now, therefore, be more distinctly seen, and by taking advantage of these we succeeded in making a few miles of westing, the "leads" taking us more in-shore, towards Admiralty Inlet, than before. Towards sunset we became more and more hampered, and were eventually beset during the night. A breeze sprang up from the westward, which increasing to a fresh gale, we found ourselves at daylight far to the eastward, and also within two miles of the land, near a long low point, which on the former voyages had not been seen. The sea was covered with ice between us and the shore, all of this year's formation, but now of considerable thickness and formidable appearance. The wind continuing strong, the whole body was constantly pressed in upon the land, p. 19bearing the ships along with it, and doubling one sheet over another, sometimes to a hundred thicknesses. We quickly shoaled the water from seventy to forty fathoms, the latter depth occurring about a mile from the beach; and after this we drifted but little, the ice being blocked up between the point and a high perpendicular berg lying aground off it.

The sails being furled, and the top-gallant yards got down, we now considered ourselves fortunate in our situation; for had we been only a quarter of a mile farther out we should have been within the influence of a current that was there sweeping the whole body of ice to the eastward, at the rate of a mile and a half an hour. Indeed, at times this current was disposed to approach us still nearer, carrying away pieces of ice close to our quarter; but by means of long hawsers, secured to the heaviest and most compact of the small floes in-shore of us, we contrived to hold on. Under such circumstances, it evidently became expedient to endeavour, by sawing, to get the ships as close in-shore as possible, so as to secure them either to grounded ice or by anchoring within the shelter of a bay at no great distance inside of us; for it now seemed not unlikely that winter was about to put a premature stop to all further operations at sea for this season. At all events it was necessary to consult the immediate safety of the ships, and to keep them from being drifted back to the eastward. I therefore gave orders for endeavouring to get the ships in towards the bay by cutting through what level floes still remained. At the same time an officer was despatched to examine the shore, which was found safe, with regular soundings in every part. So strong had been the pressure while the ice was forcing in upon us, that on the 20th, p. 20after liberating the *Hecla* on one side, she was as firmly cemented to it on the other as after a winter's formation, and we could only clear her by heavy and repeated "sallying." After cutting in two or three hundred yards, while the people were at dinner on the 21st, our canal closed, by the external pressure coming upon the parts which we had weakened, and in a few minutes the whole was once more in motion, or, as the seamen not inaptly expressed it, "alive," mass doubling under mass, and raising those which were uppermost to a considerable height. The ice thus pressed together was now about ten feet in thickness in some places, and on an average not less than four or five, so that while thus forced in upon a ship, although soft in itself, it caused her to tremble exceedingly; a sensation, indeed, commonly experienced in forcing through young ice of considerable thickness. We were now once more obliged to be quiet spectators of what was going on around us, having with extreme difficulty succeeded in saving most of our tools that were lying on the ice when the squeezing suddenly began. Towards evening we made fast to a stationary floe, at the distance of one mile from the beach, in eighteen fathoms, where we remained tolerably quiet for the night, the ice outside of us, and as far as we could see, setting constantly at a great rate to the eastward. Some of our gentlemen, who had landed in the course of the day, and who had to scramble their way on board over the ice in motion, described the bay as deeper than it appeared from the offing. Dr. Neill "found, on such parts of the beach as were not covered with ice or snow, fragments of bituminous shale, flinty slate, and iron-stone, interspersed amongst a blue-coloured limestone gravel. As far as he was able to travel inland, the surface was p. 21composed of secondary limestone, partially covered with a thin layer of calc-sinter. From the scantiness of the vegetation here, the limestone seemed likely to contain a large proportion of magnesia. Dr. Neill was about to examine for coal, which the formation led him to expect, when the ice was observed to be in motion, obliging him hastily to return on board." Lieutenant Ross "found, about two-thirds up a small peaked insulated hill of limestone, between three and four hundred feet above the level of the sea, several pieces of coal, which he found to burn with a clear bright flame, crackling much, and throwing off slaty splinters."

Hares' burrows were numerous on this hill; Lieutenant Ross saw two of these animals, one of which he killed. A fox was also observed in its summer dress; and these, with a pair of ravens, some wingless ducks, and several snow-buntings, were all the animals noticed at this place.

A sudden motion of the ice on the morning of the 22nd, occasioned by a change of wind to the S.E., threatened to carry us directly off the land. It was now more than ever desirable to hold on, as this breeze was likely to clear the shore, and at the same time to give us a run to the westward. Hawsers were therefore run out to the land-ice, composed of some heavy masses, almost on the beach. With the *Hecla* this succeeded, but the *Fury*, being much farther from the shore, soon began to move out with the whole body of ice, which, carrying her close to the large berg off the point, swept her round the latter, where, after great exertion, Captain Hoppner succeeded in getting clear, and then made sail to beat back to us. In the meantime the strain put upon the *Hecla's* hawsers being too great for them, they snapped one after another, p. 22and a bower-anchor was let go as a last resource. It was one of Hawkins's, with the double fluke, and immediately brought up, not merely the ship, but a large floe of young ice, which had just broken our stream-cable. All hands were sent upon the floe to cut it up ahead, and the whole operation was a novel and, at times, a fearful one; for the ice, being weakened by the cutting, would suddenly gather fresh way astern, carrying men and tools with it, while the chain-cable continued to plough through it in a manner which gave one the idea of something alive, and continually renewing its attacks. The anchor held surprisingly, and after this tremendous strain had been put upon it for above an hour, we had fairly cut the floe in two, and the ship was riding in clear water about half a mile from the shore.

I was now in hopes we should have made some progress, for a large channel of clear water was left open in-shore; a breeze blew off the land, and the temperature of the atmosphere had again risen considerably. We had not sailed five miles, however, when a westerly wind took us aback, and a most dangerous swell set directly upon the shore, obliging me immediately to stand off the land; and the *Fury* being still to the eastward of the point, I ran round it, in order to rejoin her before sunset. The current was here setting very fast to the eastward, not less, I think, in some places, than two miles an hour, so that, even in a clear sea, we had little chance of stemming it, much less beset as we were in young ice during an unusually dark night of nine or ten hours' duration, with a heavy fall of snow. The consequence was, that when we made the land on the morning of the 23rd, we had been drifted the incredible distance of eight or nine leagues during the night, finding ourselves off the Wollaston p. 23Islands at the entrance of Navy Board Inlet. We stood in under the islands to look for anchorage during the night, but the water being everywhere too deep close to the shore, we made fast at sunset to some very heavy ice upon a point, which we took to be the main land, but which Captain Hoppner afterwards found to be upon one of the islands, which are at least four in number.

After midnight on the 27th the wind began to moderate, and by degrees also drew more to the southward than before. At daylight, therefore, we found ourselves seven or eight miles from the land; but no ice was in sight, except the "sludge," of honey-like consistence, with which almost the whole sea was covered. A strong blink, extending along the eastern horizon, pointed out the position of the main body of ice, which was farther distant from the eastern shore of the inlet than I ever saw it. Being assisted by a fine working breeze, which at the same time prevented the formation of any more ice to obstruct us, we made considerable progress along the land, and at noon were nearly abreast of Jackson Inlet, which we now saw to be considerably larger than our distant view of it on the former voyage had led us to suppose. We found also that what at a distance appeared an island in the entrance was in reality a dark-looking rocky hill, on the south side. A few more tacks brought us to the entrance of Port Bowen, which for two or three days past I had determined to make our wintering-place, if, as there was but little reason to expect, we should be so fortunate as to push the ships thus far. My reasons for coming to this determination, in which Captain Hoppner's opinion also served to confirm me, will be sufficiently gathered from the operations of the preceding fortnight, which convinced me that the precarious chance p. 24of making a few miles' more progress could no longer be suffered to weigh against the evident risk now attending further attempts at navigation: a risk not confined to the mere exposure of the ships to imminent danger, or the hazard of being shut out of a winter harbour, but to one which, I may be permitted to say, we all dreaded as much as these — the too obvious probability of our once more being driven back to the eastward, should we again become hampered in the young ice. Joining to this the additional consideration that no known place of security existed to the southward on this coast, I had not the smallest hesitation in availing myself of the present opportunity to get the ships into harbour. Beating up, therefore, to Port Bowen, we found it filled with "old" and "hummocky" ice, attached to the shores on both sides, as low down as about three-quarters of a mile below Stoney Island. Here we made fast in sixty-two fathoms of water, running our hawsers far in upon the ice, in case of its breaking off at the margin.

On entering Port Bowen, I was forcibly struck with the circumstance of the cliffs on the south side of the harbour being, in many places, covered with a layer of blue transparent-looking ice, occasioned undoubtedly by the snow partially thawing there, and then being arrested by the frost, and presenting a feature very indicative of the late cold summer. The same thing was observed on all the land to which we made a near approach on the south side of Barrow's Strait this season, especially about Cape York and Eardley Bay; but as we had never been close to these parts of the shore in 1819, it did not occur to me as anything new or worthy of notice. At Port Bowen, however, which in that year was closely examined, I am quite certain that no such thing was to be p. 25seen, even in the month of August, the cliffs being then quite clear of snow, except here and there a patch of drift.

Late as we had this year been (about the middle of October) in reaching Sir James Lancaster's Sound, there would still have been time for a ship engaged in a whale-fishery to have reaped a tolerable harvest, as we met with a number of whales in every part of it, and even as far as the entrance of Port Bowen. The number registered altogether in our journals is between twenty and thirty, but I have no doubt that many more than these were seen, and that a ship expressly on the look-out for them would have found full occupation for her boats. Several which came near us were of large and "payable" dimensions. I confess, however, that had I been within the Sound, in a whaler, towards the close of so unfavourable a season as this, with the young ice forming so rapidly on the whole extent of the sea, I should not have been disposed to persevere in the fishery under circumstances so precarious, and to a ship unprepared for a winter involving such evident risk. It is probable, however, that on the outside the formation of young ice would have been much retarded by the swell; and I am inclined to believe that a season so unfavourable as this will be found of rare occurrence.

We observed a great many narwhals in different parts of Barrow's Strait, and a few walruses, and should perhaps have seen many more of both, but for the continual presence of the young ice.

p. 26CHAPTER III.

Winter Arrangements—Improvements in Warming and Ventilating the Ships—Masquerades adopted as an Amusement to the Men—Establishment of Schools—Astronomical Observations—Meteorological Phenomena.

October.—Our present winter arrangements so closely resembled, in general, those before adopted, that a fresh description of them here would prove little more than a repetition of that already contained in the narratives of our former voyages. On each succeeding occasion, however, some improvements were made which, for the benefit of those hereafter engaged in similar enterprises, it may be proper to record. For all those whose lot it may be to succeed us, sooner or later, in these inhospitable regions, may be assured that it is only by rigid and unremitted attention to these and numberless other "little things" that they can hope to enjoy the good state of health which, under the Divine blessing, it has always been our happiness, in so extraordinary a degree, to experience.

In the description I shall offer of the appearances of nature, and of the various occurrences, during this winter, I know not how I can do better than pursue a method similar to that heretofore practised, by confining myself rather to the pointing out of any difference observed in them now and formerly, than by entering on a fresh description of the actual phenomena. To those who read, as well as to those who describe, the account of a winter passed in these regions can no longer be expected to afford the interest of novelty it once possessed; more especially in a station already delineated with tolerable geographical precision on our maps, and thus, as it were, p. 27brought near to our firesides at home. Independently, indeed, of this circumstance, it is hard to conceive any one thing more like another than two winters passed in the higher latitudes of the Polar regions, except when variety happens to be afforded by intercourse with some other branch of "the whole family of man." Winter after winter, nature here assumes an aspect so much alike, that cursory observation can scarcely detect a single feature of variety. The winter of more temperate climates, and even in some of no slight severity, is occasionally diversified by a thaw, which at once gives variety and comparative cheerfulness to the prospect. But here, when once the earth is covered, all is dreary, monotonous whiteness—not merely for days or weeks, but for more than half a year together. Whichever way the eye is turned, it meets a picture calculated to impress upon the mind an idea of inanimate stillness, of that motionless torpor with which our feelings have nothing congenial; of anything, in short, but life. In the very silence there is a deadness with which a human spectator appears out of keeping. The presence of man seems an intrusion on the dreary solitude of this wintry desert, which even its native animals have for awhile forsaken.

As this general description of the aspect of nature would suit alike each winter we have passed in the ice, so also, with very little variation, might our limited catalogue of occurrences and adventures serve equally for any one of those seasons. Creatures of circumstance, we act and feel as we did before on every like occasion, and as others will probably do after us in the same situation. Whatever difference time or events may have wrought in individual feelings, and however different the occupations which those feelings may have suggested, p. 28they are not such as, without impertinence, can be intruded upon others; with these "the stranger intermeddleth not." I am persuaded, therefore, that I shall be excused in sparing the dulness of another winter's diary, and confining myself exclusively to those facts which appear to possess any scientific interest, to the few incidents which did diversify our confinement, and to such remarks as may contribute to the health and comfort of any future sojourners in these dreary regions.

It may well be supposed that, in this climate, the principal desideratum which art is called upon to furnish for the promotion of health, is warmth, as well in the external air as in the inhabited apartments. Exposure to a cold atmosphere, when the body is well clothed, produces no bad effect whatever beyond a frost-bitten cheek, nose, or finger. As for any injury to healthy lungs from the breathing of cold air, or from sudden changes from this into a warm atmosphere, or *vice versb*, it may with much confidence be asserted that, with due attention to external clothing, there is nothing in this respect to be apprehended. This inference, at least, would appear legitimate, from the fact that our crews, consisting of one hundred and twenty persons, have for four winters been constantly undergoing, for months together, a change of from eighty to a hundred degrees of temperature, in the space of time required for opening two doors (perhaps less than half a minute), without incurring any pulmonary complaints at all. Nor is a covering for the mouth at all necessary under these circumstances, though to most persons very conducive to comfort; for some individuals, from extreme dislike to the condensation and freezing of the breath about the "comforter" generally used for this purpose, have never p. 29worn any such defence for the mouth; and this without the slightest injurious effect or uncomfortable feeling beyond that of a cold face, which becomes comparatively trifling by habit.

In speaking of the external clothing sufficient for health in this climate, it must be confessed that, in severe exposure, quite a load of woollen clothes, even of the best quality, is insufficient to retain a comfortable degree of warmth; a strong breeze carrying it off so rapidly that the sensation is that of the cold piercing through the body. A jacket made very long, like those called by seamen "pea-jackets," and lined with fur throughout, would be more effectual than twice the weight of woollen clothes, and is indeed almost weather-proof. For the prevention of lumbago, to which our seamen are especially liable, from their well-known habit of leaving their loins imperfectly clothed, every man should be strictly obliged to wear, under his outer clothes, a canvas belt a foot broad, lined with flannel, and having straps to go over the shoulder.

It is certain, however, that no precautions in clothing are sufficient to maintain health during a Polar winter, without a due degree of warmth in the apartments we inhabit. Most persons are apt to associate with the idea of warmth, something like the comfort derived from a good fire on a winter's evening at home; but in these regions the case is inconceivably different: here it is not simple comfort, but health, and therefore ultimately life, that depends upon it. The want of a constant supply of warmth is here immediately followed by a condensation of all the moisture, whether from the breath, victuals, or other sources, into abundant drops of water, very rapidly forming on all the coldest parts of the deck. A still p. 30lower temperature modifies, and perhaps improves the annoyance by converting it into ice, which again an occasional increase of warmth dissolves into water. Nor is this the amount of the evil, though it is the only visible part of it; for not only is a moist atmosphere thus incessantly kept up, but it is rendered stagnant also by the want of that ventilation which warmth alone can furnish. With an apartment in this state, the men's clothes and bedding are continually in a moist and unwholesome condition, generating a deleterious air, which there is no circulation to carry off; and whenever these circumstances combine for any length of time together, so surely may the scurvy, to say nothing of other diseases, be confidently expected to exhibit itself.

With a strong conviction of these facts, arising from the extreme anxiety with which I have been accustomed to watch every minute circumstance connected with the health of our people, it may be conceived how highly I must appreciate any means that can be devised to counteract effects so pernicious. Such means have been completely furnished by Mr. Sylvester's warming apparatus—a contrivance of which I scarcely know how to express my admiration in adequate terms. The alteration adopted on this voyage, of placing this stove in the very bottom of the hold, produced not only the effect naturally to be expected from it, of increasing the rapidity of the current of warm air, and thus carrying it to all the officers' cabins with less loss of heat in its passage; but was also accompanied by an advantage scarcely less important, which had *not* been anticipated. This was the perfect and uniform warmth maintained during the winter in both cable-tiers, which, when cleared of all the stores, gave us another habitable deck, on which more p. 31than one-third of the men's hammocks were berthed, thus affording to the ships' companies, during seven or eight months of the year, the indescribable comfort of nearly twice the space for their beds, and twice the volume of air to breathe in. It need scarcely be added, how conducive to wholesome ventilation, and to the prevention of moisture below, such an arrangement proved; suffice it to say, that we have never before been so free from moisture, and that I cannot but chiefly attribute to this apparatus the unprecedented good state of health we enjoyed during this winter.

Every attention was, as usual, paid to the occupation and diversion of the men's minds, as well as to the regularity of their bodily exercise. Our former amusements being almost worn threadbare, it required some ingenuity to devise any plan that should possess the charm of novelty to recommend it. This purpose was completely answered, however, by a proposal of Captain Hoppner, to attempt a masquerade, in which officers and men should alike take part, but which, without imposing any restraint whatever, would leave every one to their own choice, whether to join in this diversion or not. It is impossible that any idea could have proved more happy or more exactly suited to our situation. Admirably dressed characters of various descriptions readily took their parts, and many of these were supported with a degree of spirit and genuine humour which would not have disgraced a more refined assembly; while the latter might not have disdained, and would not have been disgraced by copying the good order, decorum, and inoffensive cheerfulness which our humble masquerades presented. It does especial credit to the dispositions and good sense of our men that, though all the officers entered p. 32fully into the spirit of these amusements, which took place once a month alternately on board each ship, no instance occurred of anything that could interfere with the regular discipline, or at all weaken the respect of the men towards their superiors. Ours were masquerades without licentiousness—carnivals without excess.

But an occupation not less assiduously pursued, and of infinitely more eventual benefit, was furnished by the re-establishment of our schools, under the voluntary superintendence of my friend Mr. Hooper in the *Hecla*, and of Mr. Mogg in the *Fury*. By the judicious zeal of Mr. Hooper, the *Hecla's* school was made subservient, not merely to the improvement of the men in reading and writing (in which, however, their progress was surprisingly great), but also to the cultivation of that religious feeling which so essentially improves the character of a seaman, by furnishing the highest motives for increased attention to every other duty. Nor was the benefit confined to the eighteen or twenty individuals whose want of scholarship brought them to the school-table, but extended itself to the rest of the ship's company, making the whole lower-deck such a scene of quiet, rational occupation as I never before witnessed on board a ship. And I do not speak lightly, when I express my thorough persuasion that to the moral effects thus produced upon the minds of the men were owing, in a very high degree, the constant yet sober cheerfulness, the uninterrupted good order, and even, in some measure, the extraordinary state of health which prevailed among us during this winter.

Immediately after the ships were finally secured, we erected the observatory on shore, and commenced our arrangements for the various observations to which our p. 33attention was to be directed during the winter. The interest of these, especially of such as related to magnetism, increased so much as we proceeded, that the neighbourhood of the observatory assumed ere long almost the appearance of a scattered village, the number of detached houses, having various needles set up in them, soon amounting to seven or eight.

The extreme facility with which sounds are heard at a considerable distance in severely cold weather has often been a subject of remark; but a circumstance occurred at Port Bowen which deserves to be noticed, as affording a sort of measure of this facility, or at least conveying to others some definite idea of the fact. Lieutenant Foster, having occasion to send a man from the observatory to the opposite shore of the harbour, a measured distance of 6696 feet, or about one statute mile and two-tenths, in order to fix a meridian mark, had placed a second person half-way between to repeat his directions; but he found, on trial, that this precaution was unnecessary, as he could without difficulty keep up a conversation with the man at the distant station. The thermometer was at this time -180, the barometer 30.14 inches, and the weather nearly calm, and quite clear and serene.

The meteorological phenomena observed during this winter, like most of its other occurrences, differed so little in character from those noticed on the former voyages, as to render a separate description of each wholly unnecessary.

This winter certainly afforded but few brilliant displays of the Aurora. The following notice includes all that appear to me to require a separate description.

Late on the night of the 21st of December the phenomenon appeared partially, and with a variable light, p. 34in different parts of the southern sky for several hours. At seven on the following morning it became more brilliant and stationary, describing a well-defined arch, extending from the E.S.E. horizon to that at W.N.W., and passing through the zenith. A very faint arch was also visible on each side of this, appearing to diverge from the same points in the horizon, and separating to twenty degrees distance in the zenith. It remained thus for twenty minutes, when the coruscations from each arch met, and after a short but brilliant display of light, gradually died away. Early on the morning of the 15th of January, 1825, the Aurora broke out to the southward, and continued variable for three hours, between a N.W. and S.E. bearing. From three to four o'clock the whole horizon, from south to west, was brilliantly illuminated, the light being continuous almost throughout the whole extent, and reaching several degrees in height. Very bright vertical rays were constantly shooting upwards from the general mass. At half-past five it again became so brilliant as to attract particular notice, describing two arches passing in an east and west direction, very near the zenith, with bright coruscations issuing from it; but the whole gradually disappeared with the returning dawn. At dusk the same evening, the Aurora again appeared in the southern quarter, and continued visible nearly the whole night, but without any remarkable feature.

About midnight on the 27th of January, this phenomenon broke out in a single compact mass of brilliant yellow light, situated about a S.E. bearing, and appearing only a short distance above the land. This mass of light, notwithstanding its general continuity, sometimes appeared to be evidently composed of numerous pencils of p. 35rays, compressed, as it were, laterally into one, its limits both to the right and left being well defined and nearly vertical. The light, though very bright at all times, varied almost constantly in intensity, and this had the appearance (not an uncommon one in the Aurora) of being produced by one volume of light overlaying another, just as we see the darkness and density of smoke increased by cloud rolling over cloud. While Lieutenants Sherer and Ross, and myself, were admiring the extreme beauty of this phenomenon from the observatory, we all simultaneously uttered an exclamation of surprise at seeing a bright ray of the Aurora shoot suddenly downward from the general mass of light, and between us and the land, which was there distant only three thousand yards. Had I witnessed this phenomenon by myself, I should have been disposed to receive with caution the evidence even of my own senses, as to this last fact; but the appearance conveying precisely the same idea to three individuals at once, all intently engaged in looking towards the spot, I have no doubt that the ray of light actually passed within that distance of us.

About one o'clock on the morning of the 23rd of February, the Aurora again appeared over the hills in a south direction, presenting a brilliant mass of light, very similar to that just described. The rolling motion of the light laterally was here also very striking, as well as the increase of its intensity thus occasioned. The light occupied horizontally about a point of the compass, and extended in height scarcely a degree above the land, which seemed, however, to conceal from us a part of the phenomenon. It was always evident enough that the most attenuated light of the Aurora sensibly dimmed the p. 36stars, like a thin veil drawn over them. We frequently listened for any sound proceeding from this phenomenon, but never heard any. Our variation-needles, which were extremely light, suspended in the most delicate manner, and from the weak directive energy susceptible of being acted upon by a very slight disturbing force, were never in a single instance sensibly affected by the Aurora, which could scarcely fail to have been observed at some time or other, had any such disturbance taken place, the needles being visited every hour for several months, and oftener, when anything occurred to make it desirable.

The meteors called Falling-stars were much more frequent during this winter than we ever before saw them, and particularly during the month of December. On the 8th, at a quarter past seven in the evening, a particularly large and brilliant meteor of this kind fell in the S.S.W., the weather being very fine and clear overhead, but hazy near the horizon. On the following day, between four and five P.M., another very brilliant one was observed in the north, falling from an altitude of about thirty-five degrees till lost behind the land; the weather was at this time clear and serene, and no remarkable change took place. On the 12th, no less than five meteors of this kind were observed in a quarter of an hour, and as these were attended with some remarkable circumstances, I shall here give the account furnished me by Mr. Ross, who with Mr. Bell observed these phenomena. "From seven to nine P.M. the wind suddenly increased from a moderate breeze to a strong gale from the southward. At ten it began to moderate a little; the haze, which had for several hours obscured every star, gradually sinking towards the horizon, and by p. 37eleven o'clock the whole atmosphere was extremely clear above the altitude of five or six degrees. The thermometer also fell from -50 to -90 as the haze cleared away. At a quarter past eleven my attention was directed by Mr. Bell to some meteors which he observed, and in less than a quarter of an hour five were seen. The two first, noticed only by Mr. Bell, fell in quick succession, probably not more than two minutes apart. The third appeared about eight minutes after these, and exceeded in brilliancy any of the surrounding stars. It took a direction from near β Tauri, and passing slowly towards the Pleiades, left behind it sparks like the tail of a rocket, these being visible for a few seconds after the meteor appeared to break, which it did close to the Pleiades. The fourth meteor made its appearance very near the same place as the last, and about five minutes after it. Taking the course of those seen by Mr. Bell, it passed to the eastward, and disappeared half way between β Tauri and Gemini. The fifth of these meteors was seen to the eastward, passing through a space of about five degrees from north to south parallel to the horizon, and moving along the upper part of the cloud of haze which still extended to the altitude of five or six degrees. It was more dim than the rest, and of a red colour like Aldebaran. The third of these meteors was the only one that left a tail behind it, as above described. There was a faint appearance of the Aurora to the westward near the horizon.

On the 14th of December several very bright meteors were observed to fall between the hours of five and six in the evening, at which time the wind freshened from the N.W. by N. in a very remarkable manner. On this occasion, as well as on the 12th of December, there p. 38appeared to be an evident coincidence between the occurrence of the meteors and the changes of the weather at the time.

Particular attention was paid to the changes in the barometer during this winter, to which much encouragement was given by the excellence of the instruments with which we were now furnished. The times of register at sea had been three and nine, A.M. and P.M.; those hours having been recommended as the most proper for detecting any horary oscillations of the mercurial column. When we were fixed for the winter, and our attention could be more exclusively devoted to scientific objects, the register was extended to four and ten, and subsequently to five and eleven o'clock. The most rigid attention to the observation and correction of the column, during several months, discovered an oscillation amounting only to ten thousandth-parts of an inch. The times of the maximum and minimum altitude appear, however, decidedly to lean to four and ten o'clock, and to follow a law directly the reverse, as to time, of that found to obtain in temperate climates, the column being highest at four, and lowest at ten o'clock, both A.M. and P.M.

The barometer did not appear to indicate beforehand the changes of the weather with any degree of certainty. Indeed the remark that we had always before made, that alterations in the mercurial column more frequently accompany than precede the visible changes of weather in these regions, was equally true of our present experience; but on one or two occasions hard gales of considerable duration occurred without the barometer falling at all below the mean altitude of the column in these regions, or even rose steadily during the continuance of the gale. p. 39During one week of almost constant blowing weather, and two days of very violent gales from the eastward, in the month of April, the barometer remained considerably above thirty inches the whole time. It is necessary for me here to remark that the unusual proportion of easterly winds registered in our journals during this winter must, in my opinion, be attributed to the local situation of our winter-quarters, which alone appears to me sufficient to account for the anomaly. The lands on each side of Port Bowen, running nearly east and west, and rising to a height of six to nine hundred feet above the sea, with deep and broad ravines intersecting the country in almost every direction, may be supposed to have had considerable influence on the direction of the wind. In confirmation of this supposition, indeed, it was usually noticed that the easterly winds were with us attended with clear weather, while the contrary obtained with almost every breeze from the west and north-west, thus reversing in this respect also the usual order of things. It was moreover observed that the clouds were frequently coming from the north-west, when the wind in Port Bowen was easterly. I must, however, except the gales we experienced from the eastward, which were probably strong enough to overcome any local deflection to which a light breeze would be subject; and indeed these were always accompanied with overcast weather and a high thermometer. After the middle of October the gales of wind were very few till towards the middle of April, when we experienced more blowing weather than during the whole winter.

p. 40CHAPTER IV.

Meteorological Phenomena continued—Re-equipment of the Ships—Several Journeys undertaken—Open Water in the Offing—Commence sawing a Canal to liberate the Ships—Disruption of the Ice—Departure from Port Bowen.

The height of the land about Port Bowen deprived us longer than usual of the sun's presence above our horizon. Some of our gentlemen, indeed, who ascended a high hill for the purpose, caught a glimpse of him on the 2nd of February; on the 15th it became visible at the observatory, but at the ships not till the 22nd, after an absence of one hundred and twenty-one days. It is very long after the sun's reappearance in these regions, however, that the effect of his rays, as to warmth, becomes perceptible; week passes after week with scarcely any rise in the thermometer except for an hour or two during the day; and it is at this period more than any other, perhaps, that the lengthened duration of a polar winter's cold is most wearisome, and creates the most impatience. Towards the third week in March, thin flakes of snow lying upon black painted wood or metal, and exposed to the sun's direct rays in a sheltered situation, readily melted. In the second week of April any very light covering of sand or ashes upon the snow close to the ships might be observed to make its way downward into holes; but a coat of sand laid upon the unsheltered ice, to the distance of about two-thirds of a mile, for dissolving a canal to hasten our liberation, produced no such sensible effect till the beginning of May. Even then the dissolution was very trifling till about the first week in June, when pools of water began to make their appearance, and not long p. 41after this a small boat would have floated down it. On shore the effect is in general still more tardy, though some deception is there occasioned by the dissolution of the snow next the ground, while its upper surface is to all appearance undergoing little or no change. Thus a greater alteration is sometimes produced in the aspect of the land by a single warm day in an advanced part of the season than in many weeks preceding, in consequence of the last crust of snow being dissolved, leaving the ground at length entirely bare. We could now perceive the snow beginning to leave the stones from day to day as early as the last week in April. Towards the end of May a great deal of snow was dissolved daily, but owing to the porous nature of the ground, which absorbed it as fast as it was formed, it was not easy to procure water for drinking on shore, even as late as the 10th of June. In the ravines, however, it could be heard trickling under stones before that time, and about the 18th, many considerable streams were formed, and constantly running both night and day. After this, the thawing proceeded at an inconceivably rapid rate, the whole surface of the floes being covered with large pools of water rapidly increasing in size and depth.

We observed nothing extraordinary with respect to the sun's light about the shortest day; but as early as the 20th of November Arcturus could very plainly be distinguished by the naked eye, when near the south meridian at noon. About the first week in April the reflection of light from the snow became so strong as to create inflammation in the eyes, and notwithstanding the usual precaution of wearing black crape veils during exposure, several cases of snow-blindness occurred shortly afterwards.

There are perhaps few things more difficult to obtain p. 42than a comparative measure of the quantity of snow that falls at different places, owing to the facility with which the wind blows it off a smooth surface, such as a floe of level ice, and the collection occasioned by drift in consequence of the smallest obstruction. Thus, its mean depth at Port Bowen, measured in twenty different places on the smooth ice of the harbour, was three inches on the 5th of April, and on the 1st of May it had only increased to four and a half inches, while an immense bank, fourteen feet deep, had formed on one side of the *Hecla*, occasioned by the heavy drifts. The crystals were, as usual, extremely minute during the continuance of the cold weather, and more or less of these were always falling, even on the clearest days.

The animals seen at Port Bowen may now be briefly noticed. The principal of those seen during the winter were bears, of which we killed twelve, from October to June, being more than during all the other voyages taken together; and several others were seen. One of these animals was near proving fatal to a seaman of the *Fury*, who, having straggled from his companions, when at the top of a high hill saw a large bear coming towards him. Being unarmed, he prudently made off, taking off his boots to enable him to run the faster, but not so prudently precipitated himself over an almost perpendicular cliff, down which he was said to have rolled or fallen several hundred feet; here he was met by some of the people in so lacerated a condition as to be in a very dangerous state for some time after.

A she-bear, killed in the open water on our first arrival at Port Bowen, afforded a striking instance of maternal affection in her anxiety to save her two cubs. She might herself easily have escaped the boat, but would not p. 43forsake her young, which she was actually "towing" off by allowing them to rest on her back, when the boat came near them. A second similar instance occurred in the spring, when two cubs having got down into a large crack in the ice their mother placed herself before them, so as to secure them from the attacks of our people, which she might easily have avoided herself.

This unusual supply of bear's flesh was particularly serviceable as food for the Esquimaux dogs we had brought out, and which were always at work in a sledge; especially as, during the winter, our number was increased by the birth of six others of these useful animals.

One or two foxes (*Canis Lagopus*) were killed, and four caught in traps during the winter, weighing from four pounds and three-quarters to three pounds and three-quarters. The colour of one of these animals, which lived for some time on board the *Fury* and became tolerably tame, was nearly pure white till the month of May, when he shed his winter-coat and became of a dirty chocolate colour, with two or three light brown spots. Only three hares (*Lepus Variabilis*) were killed from October to June, weighing from six to eight pounds and three-quarters. Their fur was extremely thick, soft, and of the most beautiful whiteness imaginable. We saw no deer near Port Bowen at any season, neither were we visited by their enemies the wolves. A single ermine and a few mice (*Mus Hudsonius*) complete, I believe, our scanty list of quadrupeds at this desolate and unproductive place.

Of birds, we had a flock or two of ducks occasionally flying about the small lanes of open water in the offing, as late as the 3rd of October; but none from that time to the beginning of June, and then only a single pair was p. 44occasionally seen. A very few grouse were met with also after our arrival at Port Bowen; a single specimen was obtained on the 23rd of December, and another on the 18th of February. They again made their appearance towards the end of March, and in less than a month about two hundred were killed; after which we scarcely saw another, for what reason we could not conjecture, except that they might possibly be on their way to the northward, and that the utter barrenness of the land about Port Bowen afforded no inducement for their remaining in our neighbourhood.

Lieutenant Ross, who paid great attention to ornithology, remarked that the grouse met with here are of three kinds, namely, the ptarmigan (*Tetrao Lagopus*), the rock-grouse, (*Tetrao Rupestris*), and the willow-partridge (*Tetrao Albus*). Of these only the two former were seen in the spring, and by far the greater number killed were of the first-mentioned species. They usually had in their maws the leaves of the *Dryas Integrifolia*, buds of the *Saxifraga Oppositifolia*, *Salix Arctica*, and *Draba Alpina*, the quantities being according to the order in which the plants have here been named. A few leaves also of the *Polygonum Viviparum* were found in one or two specimens. The snow-bunting, with its sprightly note, was, as usual, one of our earliest visitants in the spring; but these were few in number and remained only a short time. A very few sand-pipers were also seen, and now and then one or two glaucous, ivory, and kittiwake gulls. A pair of ravens appeared occasionally during the whole winter here, as at most of our former winter stations.

With a view to extend our geographical knowledge as much as our means permitted, three land journeys were undertaken as soon as the weather was sufficiently warm p. 45for procuring any water. The first party, consisting of six men, under Captain Hoppner, were instructed to travel to the eastward, to endeavour to reach the sea in that direction and to discover the communication which probably exists there with Admiralty Inlet, so as to determine the extent of that portion of insular land on which Port Bowen is situated. They returned on the 14th, after a very fatiguing journey, and having with difficulty travelled a degree and three-quarters to the eastward of the ships, in latitude 730 19', from which position no appearance of the sea could be perceived. Captain Hoppner described the ravines as extremely difficult to pass, many of them being four or five hundred feet deep and very precipitous. These being numerous and running chiefly in a north and south direction, appearing to empty themselves into Jackson's Inlet, preclude the possibility of performing a quick journey to the eastward. During the whole fortnight's excursion scarcely a patch of vegetation could be seen. Indeed, the hills were so covered in most parts with soft and deep snow that a spot could seldom be found on which to pitch their tent. A few snow-buntings and some ivory gulls were all the animals they met with to enliven this most barren and desolate country; and nothing was observed in the geological character differing from that about Port Bowen.

In the bed of one of the ravines Captain Hoppner noticed some immense masses of rock, thirty or forty tons in weight, which had recently fallen from above, and he also passed over several avalanches of snow piled to a vast height across it.

The two other parties, consisting of four men each, under the respective commands of Lieutenants Sherer p. 46and Ross, were directed to travel, the former to the southward, and the latter to the northward, along the coast of Prince Regent's Inlet, for the purpose of surveying it accurately, and of obtaining observations for the longitude and variation at the stations formerly visited by us on the 7th and 15th of August, 1819. I was also very anxious to ascertain the state of the ice to the northward to enable me to form some judgment as to the probable time of our liberation.

These parties found the travelling along shore so good as to enable them not only to reach those spots, but to extend their journeys far beyond them. Lieutenant Ross returning on the 15th, brought the welcome intelligence of the sea being perfectly open and free from ice at the distance of twenty-two miles to the northward of Port Bowen, by which I concluded—what, indeed, had long before been a matter of probable conjecture,—that Barrow's Strait was not permanently frozen during the winter. From the tops of the hills about Cape York, beyond which promontory Lieutenant Ross travelled, no appearance of ice could be distinguished. Innumerable ducks, chiefly of the king, eider, and long-tailed species, were flying about near the margin of the ice, besides dovekies, looms, and glaucous, kittiwake, and ivory gulls. Lieutenant Sherer returned to the ships on the evening of the 15th, having performed a rapid journey as far as 72 p. 47fresh; but as this might in a northern climate remain the case for a number of years, and as our board erected in 1819 was still standing untouched and in good order, it is certain these people had not been here since our former visit. Less numerous traces of the Esquimaux, and of older date, occur near Port Bowen and in Lieutenant Ross's route along shore to the northward, and a few of the remains of habitations were those used as winter residences. I have since regretted that Lieutenant Sherer was not furnished with more provisions and a larger party to have enabled him to travel round Cape Kater, which is probably not far distant from some of the northern Esquimaux stations mentioned in my Journal of the preceding voyage.

Towards the end of June, the dovekies (*Colymbus Grylle*) were extremely numerous in the cracks of the ice at the entrance of Port Bowen, and as these were the only fresh supply of any consequence that we were able to procure at this unproductive place, we were glad to permit the men to go out occasionally with guns, after the ships were ready for sea, to obtain for their messes this wholesome change of diet; while such excursions also contributed essentially to their general health and cheerfulness. Many hundreds of these birds were thus obtained in the course of a few days. On the evening of the 6th of July, however, I was greatly shocked at being informed by Captain Hoppner that John Cotterell, a seaman of the *Fury*, had been found drowned in one of the cracks of the ice, by two other men belonging to the same party who had been with him but a few minutes before. We could never ascertain precisely in what manner this accident happened, but it was supposed that he must have overreached himself in stooping for a bird p. 48that he had killed. His remains were committed to the earth on Sunday the 10th, with every solemnity which the occasion demanded, and our situation would allow; and a tomb of stones with a suitable inscription was afterwards erected over the grave.

In order to obtain oil for another winter's consumption before the ships could be released from the ice, and our travelling parties having seen a number of black whales in the open water to the northward, two boats from each ship were, with considerable labour, transported four miles along shore in that direction, to be in readiness for killing a whale and boiling the oil on the beach, whenever the open water should approach sufficiently near. They took their station near a remarkable peninsular piece of land on the south side of the entrance to Jackson's Inlet, which had on the former voyage been taken for an island. Notwithstanding these preparations, however, it was vexatious to find that on the 9th of July the water was still three miles distant from the boats, and at least seven from Port Bowen. On the 12th, the ice in our neighbourhood began to detach itself, and the boats under the command of Lieutenants Sherer and Ross being launched on the following day, succeeded almost immediately in killing a small whale of "five feet bone," exactly answering our purpose. Almost at the same time, and as it turned out very opportunely, the ice at the mouth of our harbour detached itself at an old crack, and drifted off, leaving only about one mile and a quarter between us and the sea. Half of this distance being occupied by the gravelled canal, which was dissolved quite through the ice in many parts and had become very thin in all, every officer and man in both ships were set to work without delay to commence a fresh canal from the open water, to p. 49communicate with the other. This work proved heavier than we expected, the ice being generally from five to eight feet, and in many places from ten to eleven, in thickness. It was continued, however, with the greatest cheerfulness and alacrity from seven in the morning till seven in the evening daily, the dinner being prepared on the ice and eaten under the lee of a studding sail erected as a tent.

On the afternoon of the 19th a very welcome stop was put to our operations by the separation of the floe entirely across the harbour, and about one-third from the ships to where we were at work. All hands being instantly recalled by signal, were on their return set to work to get the ships into the gravelled canal, and to saw away what still remained in it to prevent our warping to sea. This work, with only half an hour's intermission for the men's supper, was continued till half-past six the following morning, when we succeeded in getting clear. The weather being calm, two hours were occupied in towing the ships to sea, and thus the officers and men were employed at very laborious work for twenty-six hours, during which time there were, on one occasion, fifteen of them overboard at once; and, indeed, several individuals met with the same accident three times. It was impossible, however, to regret the necessity of these comparatively trifling exertions, especially as it was now evident that to have sawed our way out, without any canal, would have required at least a fortnight of heavy and fatiguing labour.

p. 50CHAPTER V.

Sail over towards the Western Coast of Prince Regent's Inlet—Stopped by the Ice—Reach the Shore about Cape Seppings—Favourable Progress along the Land—Fresh and repeated Obstructions from Ice—Both Ships driven on Shore—Fury seriously damaged—Unsuccessful Search for a Harbour for heaving her down to repair.

July 20.—On standing out to sea, we sailed with a light southerly wind towards the western shore of Prince Regent's Inlet, which it was my first wish to gain, on account of the evident advantage to be derived from coasting the southern part of that portion of land called in the chart "North Somerset," as far as it might lead to the westward; which, from our former knowledge, we had reason to suppose it would do as far at least as the longitude of 950, in the parallel of about 720. After sailing about eight miles, we were stopped by a body of close ice lying between us and a space of open water beyond. By way of occupying the time in further examination of the state of the ice, we then bore up with a light northerly wind, and ran to the south-eastward to see if there was any clear water between the ice and the land in that direction; but found that there was no opening between them to the southward of the flat-topped hill laid down in the chart, and now called Mount Sherer. Indeed, I believe that at this time the ice had not yet detached itself from the land to the southward of that station. On standing back, we were shortly after enveloped in one of the thick fogs which had, for several weeks past, been observed almost daily hanging over some part of the sea in the offing, though we had scarcely experienced any in Port Bowen until the water became open at the mouth of the harbour.

p. 51On the clearing up of the fog on the 21st, we could perceive no opening of the ice leading towards the western land; nor any appearance of the smallest channel to the southward along the eastern shore. I was determined, therefore, to try at once a little farther to the northward, the present state of the ice appearing completely to accord with that observed in 1819, its breadth increasing as we advanced from Prince Leopold's Islands to the southward. As, therefore, I felt confident of being able to push along the shore if we should once gain it, I was anxious to effect the latter object in any part rather than incur the risk of hampering the ships by a vain, or, at least, a doubtful attempt to force them through a body of close ice several miles wide, for the sake of a few leagues of southing, which would soon be regained by coasting.

Light winds detained us very much, but being at length favoured by a breeze, we carried all sail to the north-west, the ice very gradually leading us towards the Leopold Isles. Having arrived off the northernmost on the morning of the 22nd, it was vexatious, however curious, to observe the exact coincidence of the present position of the ice with that which it occupied a little later in the year 1819. The whole body of it seemed to cling to the western shore, as if held there by some strong attraction, forbidding, for the present, any access to it. We now stood off and on, in the hope that a southerly breeze, which had just sprung up, might serve to open us a channel.

In the evening the wind gradually freshened, and before midnight had increased to a strong gale, which blew with considerable violence for ten hours, obliging us to haul off from the ice and to keep in smooth water under the eastern land until it abated; after which not a moment was lost in again standing over to the westward. p. 52After running all night, with light and variable winds, through loose and scattered ice, we suddenly found ourselves, on the clearing up of a thick fog, through which we had been sailing on the morning of the 24th, within one-third of a mile of Cape Seppings, the land just appearing above the fog in time to save us from danger, the soundings being thirty-eight fathoms, on a rocky bottom. The *Fury* being apprised by guns of our situation, both ships were hauled off the land, and the fog soon after dispersing, we had the satisfaction to perceive that the late gale had blown the ice off the land, leaving us a fine navigable channel from one to two miles wide, as far as we could see from the mast-head along the shore. We were able to avail ourselves of this but slowly, however, in consequence of a light southerly breeze still blowing against us.

We had now an opportunity of discovering that a long neck of very low land runs out from the southernmost of the Leopold Islands, and another from the shore to the southward of Cape Clarence. These two had every appearance of joining, so as to make a peninsula, instead of an island, of that portion of land which, on account of our distance preventing our seeing the low beach, had in 1819 been considered under the latter character. It is, however, still somewhat doubtful, and the Leopold Isles, therefore, still retain their original designation on the chart. The land here, when closely viewed, assumes a very striking and magnificent character, the strata of limestone, which are numerous and quite horizontally disposed, being much more regular than on the eastern shore of Prince Regent's Inlet, and retaining nearly their whole perpendicular height of six or seven hundred feet, close to the sea. The southeastern promontory of the southernmost p. 53island is particularly picturesque and beautiful, the heaps of loose *dibris* lying here and there up and down the sides of the cliff giving it the appearance of some huge and impregnable fortress, with immense buttresses of masonry supporting the walls. Near Cape Seppings, and some distance beyond it to the southward, we noticed a narrow stratum of some very white substance, the nature of which we could not at this time conjecture. I may here remark that the whole of Barrow's Strait, as far as we could see to the N.N.E. of the islands, was entirely free from ice; and from whatever circumstance it may proceed, I do not think that this part of the Polar Sea is at any season very much encumbered with it.

It was the general feeling, at this period, among us, that the voyage had but now commenced. The labours of a bad summer, and the tedium of a long winter, were forgotten in a moment when we found ourselves upon ground not hitherto explored, and with every apparent prospect before us of making as rapid a progress as the nature of this navigation will permit towards the final accomplishment of our object.

Early on the morning of the 25th, we passed the opening in the land delineated in the former chart of this coast, in latitude 730 34', which we now found to be a bay about three miles deep, but apparently open to the sea. I named it after my friend, Hastings Elwin, Esq., of Bristol, as a token of grateful esteem for that gentleman. The wind falling very light, so that the ships made no progress, I took the opportunity of landing in the fore-noon, accompanied by a party of the officers, and was soon after joined by Captain Hoppner. We found the formation to consist wholly of lime, and now discovered the nature of the narrow white stratum observed the day p. 54before from the offing, and which proved to be gypsum, mostly of the earthy kind, and some of it of a very pure white. A part of the rock near our landing-place contained a quantity of it in the state of selenite in beautiful transparent laminf of a large size. The abundance of gypsum hereabouts explained also the extreme whiteness of the water near the whole of this part of the coast, which had always been observed in approaching it, and which had at first excited unnecessary apprehensions as to the soundings along the shore. This colour is more particularly seen near the mouths of the streams, many of which are quite of a dirty milk colour, and tinge the sea to the distance of more than a mile, without any alteration in the depth, except a gradual diminution in going in. The vegetation in this place was, as usual, extremely scanty, though much more luxuriant than on any of the land near our winter quarters, and no animals were seen. The latitude of our landing-place was 730 27'

23", the longitude by chronometers 900 50' 34.6", and the variation of the magnetic needle 1250 34' 42" westerly. From half-past nine A.M. till a quarter past noon the tide fell two feet three inches; and as it was nearly stationary at the latter time, it was probably near low water.

A breeze enabling us again to make some progress, and an open channel still favouring us of nearly the same breadth as before, we passed during the night a second bay, about the same size as the other, and also appearing open to the sea; it lies in latitude (by account from the preceding and following noon) 730 19' 30", and its width is one mile and a half. It was called Batty Bay, after my friend Captain Robert Batty, of the Grenadier Guards. We now perceived that the ice closed completely in with p. 55the land a short distance beyond us, and having made all the way we could, were obliged to stand off and on during the day in a channel not three-quarters of a mile wide. This channel being still more contracted towards the evening, we were obliged to make fast to some grounded land ice upon the beach in four fathoms water, there to await some change in our favour. We here observed traces of our old friends the Esquimaux, there being several of their circles of stones, though not of recent date, close to the sea. We also found a more abundant vegetation than before, and several plants familiar to us on the former voyages, but not yet procured on this, were now added to our collections. The geological character of the land was nearly the same as before, but we found here some gypsum of the fibrous kind, occurring in a single stratum about an inch and a half wide. About a mile to the north of us was a curious cascade or spout of water, issuing from a chasm in the rock, and falling more than two hundred feet perpendicular. Our gentlemen, who visited the spot, described it as rendered the more picturesque by innumerable kittiwakes having their nests among the rocks, and constantly flying about the stream. The latitude was 730 06' 17", the longitude by chronometers 910 19' 52.3", the dip of the magnetic needle 880 02.1', and the variation 1280 23' 17" westerly.

The ice opening in the afternoon of the 27th, we cast off and run four or five miles with a northerly breeze. This wind, however, always had the effect of making the ice close the shore, while a southerly breeze as uniformly opened it, so that on this coast, as on

several others that I have known, a contrary wind—however great
the paradox may seem—proved, on the whole, the most favourable
for making progress. This circumstance is simply to be p.
56attributed to the greater abundance of open water in the parts we
have left behind (in the present instance the open sea of Barrow's
Strait) than those towards which we are going. We were once more
obliged to make fast, therefore, to some grounded ice close to the
beach, rather than run any risk of hampering the ships, and rendering them unable to take advantage of a change in our favour.

A light southerly breeze on the morning of the 28th gradually
cleared the shore, and a fresh wind from the N.W. then immediately
succeeded. We instantly took advantage of this circumstance, and
casting off at six A.M. ran eight or nine miles without obstruction,
when we were stopped by the ice, which, in a closely packed and
impenetrable body, stretched close into the shore as far as the eye
could reach from the crow's nest. Being anxious to gain every foot
of distance that we could, and perceiving some grounded ice which
appeared favourable for making fast to, just at a point where the
clear water terminated, the ships were run to the utmost extent of it,
and a boat prepared from each to examine the depth of water at the
intended anchoring place. Just as I was about to leave the *Hecla* for
that purpose, the ice was observed to be in rapid motion towards
the shore. The *Fury* was immediately hauled in by some grounded
masses, and placed to the best advantage; but the *Hecla* being more
advanced was immediately beset in spite of every exertion, and
after breaking two of the largest ice-anchors in endeavouring to
heave in to the shore, was obliged to drift with the ice, several
masses of which had fortunately interposed themselves between us
and the land. The ice slackening around us a little in the evening,
we were enabled, with considerable labour, to get to some grounded masses, where we lay much exposed, as the p. 57 *Fury* also did.
In this situation, our latitude being 720 51' 51", we saw a comparatively low point of land three or four leagues to the southward,
which proved to be near that which terminated our view of this
coast in 1819.

On the 29th, the ice being slack for a short distance, we shifted the
Hecla half a mile to the northward, into a less insecure berth. I then
walked to a broad valley facing the sea near us, where a considera-

ble stream discharged itself, and where, in passing in the ships, a large fish had been observed to jump out of the water. In hopes of finding salmon here, we tried for some time with several hand-nets, but nothing was caught or seen. In this place were a number of the Esquimaux stone circles, apparently of very old date, being quite overgrown with grass, moss, and other plants. In the neighbour-hood of these habitations the vegetation was much more luxuriant than anything of the kind we had seen before during this voyage. The state of this year's plants was now very striking, compared with those of the last, and afforded strong evidence, if any had been wanting, of the difference between the two seasons. I was particularly struck with the appearance of some moss collected by Mr. Hooper, who pointed out to me upon the same specimen the last year's miserable seeds just peeping above the leaves, while those of the present summer had already shot three-quarters of an inch beyond them. Another circumstance which we noticed about this time, and still more so as the season advanced, was the rapid progress which the warmth had already made in dissolving the last year's snow, this being always easily known by its dingy colour, and its admixture with the soil. Of the past winter's snow not a particle could be seen at the close of July on any part of p. 58this coast. These facts, together with the beautiful weather we had enjoyed for many weeks past, all tended to show that we were now favoured with an unusually fine summer. We found in this place, in the dry bed of an old stream, innumerable fossils in the limestone, principally shells and madrepore. On a hill abreast of the *Hecla*, and at an elevation of not less than three or four hundred feet above the sea, one particular spot was discovered in which the same kind of shells first found in Barrow's Strait in 1819 occurred in very great abundance and perfection, wholly detached from the lime in which for the most part they were found embedded in other places on this coast. Indeed, it was quite astonishing, in looking at the numberless fossil animal remains occurring in many of the stones, to consider the countless myriads of shell fish and marine insects which must once have existed on this shore. The cliffs next the sea, which here rise to a perpendicular height of between four and five hundred feet, were continually breaking down at this season, and adding, by falls of large masses of stone, to the slope of *dibris* lying at their foot. The ships lay so close to the shore as to be almost within the range of some of these tumbling masses, there being at high water scarcely beach enough for a person to walk along the shore. The time of high water, near the opposition of the moon this night, was between half-past eleven and midnight, being nearly the same as at Port Bowen at full and change.

The ice opening for a mile and a half along shore on the 30th, we shifted the *Hecla's* berth about that distance to the southward, chiefly to be enabled to see more distinctly round a point which before obstructed our view, though our situation, as regarded the security of the ship, was much altered for the worse. The *Fury* remained p. 59where she was, there being no second berth even so good as the bad one where she was now lying. In the afternoon it blew a hard gale, with constant rain, from the northward, the clouds indicating an easterly wind in other parts. This wind, which was always the troublesome one to us, soon brought the ice closer and closer, till it pressed with very considerable violence on both ships, though the most upon the *Fury*, which lay in a very exposed situation. The *Hecla* received no damage but the breaking of two or three hawsers, and a part of her bulwark torn away by the strain upon them. In the course of the night we had reason to suppose, by the *Fury's* heeling, that she was either on shore, or still heavily pressed by the ice from without. Early on the morning of the 31st, as soon as a communication could be effected, Captain Hoppner sent to inform me that the *Fury* had been forced on the ground, where she still lay; but that she would probably be hove off without much difficulty at high water, provided the external ice did not prevent it. I also learned from Captain Hoppner that a part of one of the propelling wheels had been destroyed, the chock through which its axis passed being forced in considerably, and the palm broken off one of the bower anchors. Most of this damage, however, was either of no very material importance, or could easily be repaired. A large party of hands from the *Hecla* being sent round to the *Fury* towards high water, she came off the ground with very little strain, so that, upon the whole, considering the situation in which the ships were lying, we thought ourselves fortunate in having incurred no very serious injury. The *Fury* was shifted a few yards into the best place that could be found, and the wind again blowing strong from the northward, the ice remained p. 60close about us. A shift of wind to the southward in the afternoon at length began gradually to slacken it, but it was not till six A.M. on the 1st of August that there appeared a prospect of making any progress. There was, at this time, a great deal of water to the southward, but between us and the channel there lay one narrow and not very close stream of ice touching the shore. A shift of wind to the northward determined me at once to take advantage of it, as nothing but a free wind seemed requisite to enable us to reach this promising channel. The signal to that effect was immediately made, but while the sails were setting, the ice, which had at first been about three-quarters of a mile distant from us, was observed to be closing the shore. The ships were cast with all expedition, in hopes of gaining the broader channel before the ice had time to shut us up. So rapid, however, was the latter in this its sudden movement, that we had but just got the ships' heads the right way, when the ice came bodily in upon us, being doubtless set in motion by a very sudden freshening of the wind almost to a gale in the course of a few minutes. The ships were now almost instantly beset, and in such a manner as to be literally helpless and unmanageable. In such cases, it must be confessed that the exertions made by heaving at hawsers or otherwise are of little more service than in the occupation they furnish to the men's minds under circumstances of difficulty; for when the ice is fairly acting against the ship, ten times the strength and ingenuity could in reality avail nothing.

The sails were, however, kept set, and as the body of ice was setting to the southward withal, we went with it some little distance in that direction. The *Hecla* after thus driving, and now and then forcing her way through p. 61the ice, in all about three-quarters of a mile, quite close to the shore, at length struck the ground forcibly several times in the space of a hundred yards, and being then brought up by it remained immovable, the depth of water under her keel abaft being sixteen feet, or about a foot less than she drew. The *Fury* continuing to drive was now irresistibly carried past us, and we escaped, only by a few feet, the damage invariably occasioned by ships coming in contact under such circumstances. She had, however, scarcely passed us a hundred yards when it was evident, by the ice pressing her in, as well as along the shore, that she must soon be stopped like the *Hecla*; and having gone about two hundred yards farther she was observed to receive a severe pressure from a large floe-piece forcing her directly against a grounded mass of ice upon the beach. After setting to the southward for an hour or two longer the ice became stationary, no open water being anywhere visible from the mast-head, and the pressure on the ships remaining undiminished during the day. Just as I had ascertained the utter impossibility of moving the *Hecla* a single foot, and that she must lie quite aground fore and aft as soon as the tide fell, I received a note from Captain Hoppner informing me that the *Fury* had been so severely "nipped" and strained as to leak a good deal, apparently about four inches an hour; that she was still heavily pressed both upon the ground and against the large mass of ice within her; that the rudder was at present very awkwardly situated; and that one boat had been much damaged. As the tide fell the *Fury's* stern, which was aground, was lifted several feet, and the *Hecla* at low water having sewed five feet forward and two abaft, we presented altogether no very pleasing or comfortable spectacle. However, about high p. 62water, the ice very opportunely slacking, the *Hecla* was hove off with great ease, and warped to a floe in the offing to which we made fast at midnight. The *Fury* was not long after us in coming off the ground, when I was in hopes of finding that any twist or strain, by which her leaks might have been occasioned, would, in some measure, have closed when she was relieved from pressure and once more fairly afloat. My disappointment and morti-fication, therefore, may in some measure be imagined, at being in-formed by telegraph, about two A.M. on the 2nd, that the water was gaining on two pumps, and that a part of the doubling had floated up. The *Hecla* having in the mean time been carried two or three miles to the southward, by the ice which was once more driving in that direction, I directed Captain Hoppner by signal to endeavour to reach the best security in-shore which the present slackness of the ice might permit, until it was possible for the *Hecla* to rejoin him. Presently after perceiving from the mast-head something like a small harbour nearly abreast of us, every effort was made to get once more towards the shore. In this the ice happily favoured us, and after making sail and one or two tacks we got in with the land, when I left the ship in a boat to sound the place and search for shel-ter. I soon had the mortification to find that the harbour which had appeared to present itself so opportunely, had not more than six or seven feet water in any part of it, the whole of its defences being composed of the stones and soil washed down by a stream which here emptied itself into the sea. From this place, indeed, where the land gradually became much lower in advancing to the southward, the whole nature of the soundings entirely altered, the water gradually shoaling in approaching the beach, so that the ships p. 63could scarcely come nearer, in most parts, than a quarter of a mile. At this distance the whole shore was more or less lined with grounded masses of ice; but after examining the soundings within more than twenty of them, in the space of about a mile, I could only find two that would allow the ships to float at low water, and that by some care in placing and keeping them there. Having fixed a flag on each berg, the usual signal for the ships taking their stations, I rowed on board the *Fury*, and found four pumps constantly going to keep the ship free, and Captain Hoppner, his officers and men, almost exhausted with the incessant labour of the last eight-and-forty hours. The instant the ships were made fast, Captain Hoppner and myself set out in a boat to survey the shore still farther south, there being a narrow lane of water about a mile in that direction; for it had now become too evident, however unwilling we might have been at first to admit the conclusion, that the *Fury* could proceed no farther without repairs, and that the nature of those repairs would in all probability involve the disagreeable, I may say the ruinous, necessity of heaving the ship down. After rowing about three-quarters of a mile we considered ourselves fortunate in arriving at a bolder part of the beach, where three grounded masses of ice, having from three to four fathoms water at low tide within them, were so disposed as to afford, with the assistance of art, something like shelter. Wild and insecure as, under other circumstances, such a place would have been thought for the purpose of heaving a ship down, we had no alternative, and therefore as little occasion as we had time for deliberation. Returning to the ships, we were setting the sails in order to run to the appointed place, when the ice closed in and prevented our p. 64moving, and in a short time there was once more no open water to be seen. We were, therefore, under the necessity of remaining in our present berths, where the smallest external pressure must inevitably force us ashore, neither ship having more than two feet of water to spare. One watch of the *Hecla's* crew were sent round to assist at the *Fury's* pumps, which required one-third of her ship's company to be constantly employed at them.

The ice coming in with considerable violence on the night of the 2nd, once more forced the *Fury* on shore, so that at low water she sewed two feet and a half. Nothing but the number and strength of the *Hecla's* hawsers prevented her sharing the same fate, for the pressure was just as much as seven of these of six inches and two stream-cables would bear. The *Fury* floated in the morning, and was enabled to haul off a little, but there was no opening of the ice to allow us to move to our intended station. The more leisure we obtained to consider the state of the *Fury*, the more apparent became the absolute, however unfortunate, necessity of heaving her down. Four pumps were required to be at work without intermission to keep her free, and this in perfectly smooth water, showing that she was, in fact, so materially injured as to be very far from seaworthy. One-third of her working men were constantly employed, as before remarked, in this laborious operation, and some of their hands had become so sore from the constant friction of the ropes, that they could hardly handle them any longer without the use of mittens, assisted by the unlaying of the ropes to make them soft. When, in addition to these circumstances, the wet state of the decks and the little room left, as well as the reduced strength for working the ship or heaving at hawsers among the ice, be p. 65considered, I believe that every seaman will admit the impracticability of pursuing this critical navigation till the *Fury* had been examined and repaired. As, therefore, not a moment could be lost we took advantage of a small lane of water deep enough for boats, which kept open within the grounded masses along the shore, to convey to the *Hecla* some of the *Fury's* dry provisions, and to land a quantity of heavy ironwork and other stores not perishable; for the moment this measure was determined on I was anxious, almost at any risk, to commence the lightening of the ship as far as our present insecurity and our distance from the shore would permit.

The wind blowing fresh from the northward, which always increased our difficulties on this coast, the ice pressed so violently upon the ships as almost to force them adrift during the night, employing our people, now sufficiently harassed by their work during the day, for two or three hours in still further increasing our security by additional hawsers. We continued landing stores from the *Fury* on the 4th, and at night a bower cable was passed round one of the grounded masses alongside of her; for if either ship had once got adrift, it is difficult to say what might have been the consequence.

At two A.M. on the 5th, the ice began to slacken near the ships, and as soon as a boat could be rowed along shore to the southward, I set out, accompanied by a second from the *Fury*, for the purpose of examining the state of our intended harbour since the recent pressure, and to endeavour to prepare for the reception of the ships by clearing out the loose ice. On my arrival there, the distance being about a mile, I found that one of the three bergs had shifted its place so materially by the late movements of the ice, as not only to alter the disposition of these masses, p. 66on which our whole dependence rested, very much for the worse, but also to destroy all confidence in their stability upon the ground. Landing upon one of the bergs to show the appointed signal for the ships to come, I perceived, about half a mile beyond us to the southward, a low point forming a little bay, with a great deal of heavy grounded ice lying off it. I immediately rowed to this, in hopes of finding something like a harbour for our purpose, but on my arrival there, had once more the mortification to find that there were not above six feet of water at low tide in any part of it, and within the grounded ice not more than twelve. Having assured myself that no security or shelter was here to be found, I immediately returned to the former place, which the *Hecla* was just reaching. The *Fury* was detained some time by a quantity of loose ice which had wedged itself in, in such a manner as to leave her no room to move outwards; but she arrived about seven o'clock, when both ships were made fast in the best berths we could find, but they were still excluded from their intended place by the quantity of ice which had fixed itself there. Within twenty minutes after our arrival, the whole body of ice again came in, entirely closing up the shore, so that our moving proved most opportune.

p. 67CHAPTER VI.

Formation of a Basin for heaving the Fury down—Landing of the Fury's Stores, and other preparations—The Ships secured within the Basin—Impediments from the pressure of the Ice—Fury hove down—Securities of the Basin destroyed by a Gale of Wind—

Preparations to tow the Fury out—Hecla re-equipped, and obliged to put to Sea—Fury again driven on Shore—Rejoin the Fury; and find it necessary finally to abandon her.

As there was now no longer room for floating the ice out of our proposed basin, all hands were immediately employed in preparing the intended securities against the incursions of the ice. These consisted of anchors carried to the beach, having bower-cables attached to them, passing quite round the grounded masses, and thus enclosing a small space of just sufficient size to admit both ships. The cables we proposed floating by means of the two hand-masts and some empty casks lashed to them as buoys, with the intention of thus making them receive the pressure of the ice a foot or two below the surface of the water. By uncommon exertions on the part of the officers and men, this laborious work was completed before night as far as was practicable until the loose ice should set out; and all the tents were set up on the beach for the reception of the *Fury's* stores.

The ice remaining quite close on the 6th, every individual in both ships, with the exception of those at the pumps, was employed in landing provisions from the *Fury*, together with the spars, boats, and everything from off her upper deck. The ice coming in, in the afternoon, with a degree of pressure which usually attended a northerly wind on this coast, twisted the *Fury's* rudder so forcibly against a mass of ice lying under her p. 68stern that it was for some hours in great danger of being damaged, and was indeed only saved by the efforts of Captain Hoppner and his officers, who, without breaking off the men from their other occupations, themselves worked at the ice-saw. On the following day, the ice remaining as before, the work was continued without intermission, and a great quantity of things landed. The two carpenters (Messrs. Pulfer and Fiddis) took the *Fury's* boats in hand themselves, their men being required as part of our physical strength in clearing the ship. The armourer was also set to work on the beach in forging bolts for the martingales of the outriggers. In short, every living creature among us was somehow or other employed, not even excepting our dogs, which were set to drag up the stores on the beach; so that our little dockyard soon exhibited the most animated scene imaginable. The quickest method of landing casks and other things not too weighty, was that adopted by Captain Hoppner, and consisted of a hawser secured to the ship's main mast-head, and set up as tight as possible to the anchor on the beach; the casks being hooked to a block traversing on this as a jack-stay, were made to run down it with great velocity. By this means more than two were got on shore for every one landed by the boats, the latter, however, being constantly employed in addition. The *Fury* was thus so much lightened in the course of the day that two pumps were now nearly sufficient to keep her free, and this number continued requisite until she was hove down. Her spirit-room was now entirely clear, and, on examination, the water was found to be rushing in through two or three holes that happened to be in the ceiling, and which were immediately plugged up. Indeed; it was now very evident that nothing but p. 69the tightness of the Fury's diagonal ceiling had so long kept her afloat, and that any ship not thus fortified within could not possibly have been kept free by the pumps.

At night, just as the people were going to rest, the ice began to move to the southward, and soon after came in towards the shore, again endangering the *Fury's* rudder, and pressing her over on her side to so alarming a degree, as to warn us that it would not be safe to lighten her much more in her present insecure situation. One of our bergs also shifted its position by this pressure, so as to weaken our confidence in the pier-heads of our intended basin; and a long "tongue" of one of them forcing itself under the *Hecla's* forefoot, while the drift-ice was also pressing her forcibly from astern, she once more sewed three or four feet forward at low water, and continued to do so, notwithstanding repeated endeavours to haul her off, for four successive tides the ice remaining so close and so much doubled under the ship, as to render it impossible to move her a single inch. Notwithstanding the state of the ice, however, we did not remain idle on the 8th, all hands being employed in unrigging the *Fury*, and landing all her spars, sails, booms, boats, and other top-weight.

The ice still continuing very close on the 9th, all hands were employed in attempting, by saws and axes, to clear the *Hecla*, which still grounded on the tongue of ice every tide. After four hours' labour, they succeeded in making four or five feet of room astern, when the ship suddenly slid down off the tongue with considerable force, and became once more afloat. We then got on shore the

Hecla's cables and hawsers for the accommodation of the *Fury's* men in our tiers during the heaving p. 70down, struck our top-masts which would be required as shores and outriggers, and, in short, continued to occupy every individual in some preparation or other. These being entirely completed at an early hour in the afternoon, we ventured to go on with the landing of the coals and provisions from the *Fury*, preferring to run the risk which would thus be incurred, to the loss of even a few hours in the accomplishment of our present object. As it very opportunely happened, however, the external ice slackened to the distance of about a hundred yards outside of us on the morning of the 10th, enabling us, by a most tedious and laborious operation, to clear the ice out of our basin piece by piece. The difficulty of this apparently simple process consisted in the heavy pressure having repeatedly doubled one mass under another—a position in which it requires great power to move them—and also by the corners locking in with the sides of the bergs. Our next business was to tighten the cables sufficiently by means of purchases, and to finish the floating of them in the manner and for the purpose before described. After this had been completed, the ships had only a few feet in length, and nothing in breadth to spare; but we had now great hopes of going on with our work with increased confidence and security. The *Fury*, which was placed inside, had something less than eighteen feet at low water; the *Hecla* lay in four fathoms, the bottom being strewed with large and small fragments of limestone.

While thus employed in securing the ships, the smoothness of the water enabled us to see in some degree the nature of the *Fury's* damage; and it may be conceived how much pain it occasioned us plainly to discover that both the stern-post and forefoot were broken and turned p. 71up on one side with the pressure. We also could perceive as far as we were able to see along the main-keel, that it was much torn, and we had therefore reason to conclude that the damage would altogether prove very serious. We also discovered that several feet of the *Hecla's* false keel were torn away abreast of the fore-chains, in consequence of her grounding forward so frequently.

The ships being now as well secured as our means permitted from the immediate danger of ice, the clearing of the *Fury* went on during the 11th with increased confidence, though greater alacrity was impossible, for nothing could exceed the spirit and zealous activity of every individual, and as things had turned out, the ice had not obliged us to wait a moment, except at the actual times of its pressure. Being favoured with fine weather, we continued our work very quickly, so that on the 12th every cask was landed and also the powder; and the spare sails and clothing put on board the *Hecla*. On the 13th we found that a mass of heavy ice, which had been aground within the *Fury*, had now floated off alongside of her at high water, still further contracting our already narrow basin, and leaving the ship no room for turning round. At the next high water, therefore, we got a purchase on it and hove it out of the way, so that at night it drifted off altogether. The coals and preserved meats were the principal things now remaining on board the *Fury*, and these we continued landing by every method we could devise as the most expeditious. The tide rose so considerably at night, new moon occurring within an hour of high water, that we were much afraid of our bergs floating: they remained firm, however, even though the ice came in with so much force as to break one of our hand-masts, p. 72a fir spar of twelve inches diameter. As the high tides and the lightening of the *Fury* now gave us sufficient depth of water for unshipping the rudders, we did so, and laid them upon the small berg astern of us, for fear of their being damaged by any pressure of the ice.

Early on the morning of the 14th, the ice slackening a little in our neighbourhood, we took advantage of it, though the people were much fagged, to tighten the cables, which had stretched and yielded considerably by the late pressure. It was well that we did so; for in the course of this day we were several times interrupted in our work by the ice coming with a tremendous strain on the north cables, the wind blowing strong from the N.N.W., and the whole "pack" outside of us setting rapidly to the southward. Indeed, notwithstanding the recent tightening and readjustment of the cables, the bight was pressed in so much as to force the *Fury* against the berg astern of her twice in the course of the day. Mr. Waller, who was in the hold the second time that this occurred, reported that the coals about the keelson were moved by it, imparting the sensation of a part of the ship's bottom falling down; and one of the men at work there was so strongly impressed with that belief that he thought it high time to make a spring for the hatchway. From this circumstance it seemed more than probable that the main keel had received some serious damage near the middle of the ship.

From this trial of the efficacy of our means of security, it was plain that the *Fury* could not possibly be hove down under circumstances of such frequent and imminent risk; I therefore directed a fourth anchor, with two additional cables, to be carried out, with the hope p. 73of breaking some of the force of the ice by its offering a more oblique resistance than the other, and thus by degrees turning the direction of the pressure from the ships. We had scarcely completed this new defence, when the largest floe we had seen since leaving Port Bowen came sweeping along the shore, having a motion to the southward of not less than a mile and a half an hour; and a projecting point of it just grazing our outer berg, threatened to overturn it, and would certainly have dislodged it from its situation but for the cable recently attached to it. A second similar occurrence took place with a smaller mass of ice about midnight, and near the top of an unusually high spring tide, which seemed ready to float away every security from us. For three hours about the time of this high water, our situation was a most critical one, for had the bergs, or indeed any one of them, been carried away or broken, both ships must inevitably have been driven on shore by the very next mass of ice that should come in. Happily, however, they did not suffer any further material disturbance, and the main body keeping at a short distance from the land until the tide had fallen, the bergs seemed to be once more firmly resting on the ground. The only mischief, therefore, occasioned by this disturbance was the slackening of our cables by the alteration in the positions of the several grounded masses, and the consequent necessity of employing more time, which nothing but absolute necessity could induce us to bestow in adjusting and tightening the whole of them afresh.

The wind veering to the W.N.W. on the morning of the 15th, and still continuing to blow strong, the ice was forced three or four miles off the land in the course of p. 74a few hours, leaving us a quiet day for continuing our work, but exciting no very pleasing sensations when we considered what progress we might have been making had we been at liberty to pursue our object. The land was, indeed, so clear of ice to the southward that Dr. Neill, who walked a considerable distance in that direction, could see nothing but an open channel in-shore to the utmost extent of his view. We took advantage of this open water to send the launch for the *Fury's* ironwork left at the former station; for though the few men thus employed could very ill be spared, we were obliged to arrange everything with reference to the ultimate saving of time; and it would have occupied both ships' companies more than a whole day to carry the things round by land.

The *Fury* being completely cleared at an early hour on the 16th, we were all busily employed in "winding" the ship, and in preparing the outriggers, shores, purchases, and additional rigging. Though we purposely selected the time of high water for turning the ship round, we had scarcely a foot of space to spare for doing it, and indeed, as it was, her forefoot touched the ground, and loosened the broken part of the wood so much as to enable us to pull it up with ropes, when we found the fragments to consist of the whole of the "gripe" and most of the "cutwater." The strong breeze continuing, and the sea rising as the open water increased in extent, our bergs were sadly washed and wasted; every hour producing a sensible and serious diminution in their bulk. As, however, the main body of ice still kept off, we were in hopes, now that our preparations were so near completed, we should have been enabled in a few hours to see the extent of the damage, and repair it sufficiently to p. 75allow us to proceed. In the evening we received the *Fury's* crew on board the *Hecla*, every arrangement and regulation having been previously made for their personal comfort, and for the preservation of cleanliness, ventilation, and dry warmth throughout the ship. The officers of the *Fury*, by their own choice, pitched a tent on shore for messing and sleeping in, as our accommodation for two sets of officers was necessarily confined. On the 17th, when every preparation was completed, the cables were found again so slack, by the wasting of the bergs in consequence of the continued sea, and possibly also in part by the masses having moved somewhat in-shore, that we were obliged to occupy several hours in putting them to rights, as we should soon require all our strength at the purchases. One berg had also, at the last low water, fallen over on its side in consequence of its substance being undermined by the sea, and the cable surrounding it was thus forced so low under water as no longer to afford protection from the ice should it again come in. In tightening the cables, we found it to have the effect of bringing the bergs in towards the shore, still further contracting our narrow basin; but anything was better than suffering them to go adrift. This work being finished at ten P.M. the people were allowed three hours' rest only, it being necessary to heave the ship down at or near high water, as there was not sufficient depth to allow her to take her distance at any other time of tide. Every preparation being made, at three A.M. on the 18th, we began to heave her down on the larboard side, but when the purchases were nearly a-block, we found that the strops under the *Hecla'a* bottom, as well as some of the *Fury's* shorefasts, had stretched or yielded so much, that they could not bring p. 76the keel out of water within three or four feet. We immediately eased her up again, and readjusted everything as requisite, hauling her farther in-shore than before by keeping a considerable heel upon her, so as to make less depth of water necessary; and we were then in the act of once more heaving her down, when a snowstorm came on and blew with such violence off the land, as to raise a considerable sea. The ships had now so much motion as to strain the gear very much, and even to make the lower masts of the *Fury* bend in spite of the shores: we were, therefore, most unwillingly compelled to desist until the sea should go down, keeping everything ready to recommence the instant we could possibly do so with safety. The officers and men were now literally so harassed and fatigued as to be scarcely capable of further exertion without some rest; and on this and one or two other occasions, I noticed more than a single instance of stupor amounting to a certain degree of failure in intellect, rendering the individual so affected quite unable at first to comprehend the meaning of an order, though still as willing as ever to obey it. It was therefore perhaps a fortunate necessity which produced the intermission of labour which the strength of every individual seemed to require.

The gale rather increasing than otherwise during the whole day and night of the 18th, had on the following morning, when the wind and sea still continued unabated, so destroyed the bergs on which our sole dependence was placed, that they no longer remained aground at low water; the cables had again become slack about them, and the basin we had taken so much pains in forming had now lost all its defences, at least during a portion of every tide. It will be plain, too, if I have succeeded in p. 77giving a distinct description of our situation, that, independently of the security of the ships, there was now nothing left to seaward by which the *Hecla* could be held out in that direction while heaving the *Fury* down, so that our preparations in this way were no longer available. After a night of most anxious consideration and consultation with Captain Hoppner, who was now my messmate in the *Hecla*, it appeared but too plain, that, should the ice again come in, neither ship could any longer be secured from driving on shore. It was therefore determined instantly to prepare the *Hecla* for sea, making her thoroughly effective in every respect; so that we might at least push her out into comparative safety among the ice, when it closed again, taking every person on board her, securing the *Fury* in the best manner we could, and returning to her the instant we were able to do so, to endeavour to get her out, and to carry her to some place of security for heaving down. If, after the *Hecla* was ready, time should still be allowed us, it was proposed immediately to put into the *Fury* all that was requisite, or at least as much as she could safely carry, and towing her out into the ice, to try the effect of "foddering" the leaks by sails under those parts of her keel which we knew to be damaged, until some more effectual means could be resorted to.

Having communicated to the assembled officers and ships' companies my views and intentions, and moreover given them to understand that I hoped to see the *Hecla's* top-gallant-yards across before we slept, we commenced our work; and such was the hearty goodwill and indefatigable energy with which it was carried on, that by midnight the whole was accomplished, and a bower-anchor and cable carried out in the offing, for the double p. 78purpose of hauling out the *Hecla* when requisite, and as some security to the *Fury*, if we were obliged to leave her. The people were once more quite exhausted by these exertions, especially those belonging to the *Fury*, who had never thoroughly recovered their first fatigues. The ice being barely in sight, we were enabled to enjoy seven hours of undisturbed rest; but the wind becoming light, and afterwards shifting to the N.N.E., we had reason to expect the ice would soon close the shore, and were, therefore, most anxious to continue our work.

On the 20th, therefore, the reloading of the *Fury* commenced with recruited strength and spirits, such articles being in the first place selected for putting on board as were essentially requisite for her re-equipment; for it was my full determination, could we succeed in completing this, not to wait even for rigging a topmast, or getting a lower yard up, in the event of the ice coming in, but to tow her out among the ice, and there put everything sufficiently to rights for carrying her to some place of security. At the same time, the end of the sea-cable was taken on board the *Fury*, by way of offering some resistance to the ice, which was now more plainly seen, though still about five miles distant, A few hands were also spared, consisting chiefly of two or three convalescents, and some of the officers, to thrum a sail for putting under the *Fury's* keel; for we were very anxious to relieve the men at the pumps, which constantly required the labour of eight to twelve hands to keep her free. In the course of the day, several heavy masses of ice came drifting by with a breeze from the N.E., which is here about two points upon the land, and made a considerable swell. One mass came in contact with our bergs, which, though only held by the cables, brought it up in time to p. 79prevent mischief. By a long and hard day's labour, the people not going to rest till two o'clock on the morning of the 21st, we got about fifty tons' weight of coals and provisions on board the *Fury*, which, in case of necessity, we considered sufficient to give her stability. While we were thus employed, the ice, though evidently inclined to come in, did not approach us much; and it may be conceived with what anxiety we longed to be allowed one more day's labour, on which the ultimate saving of the ship might almost be considered as depending. Having hauled the ships out a little from the shore and prepared the *Hecla* for casting by a spring at a moment's notice, all the people except those at the pumps were sent to rest, which, however, they had not enjoyed for two hours, when at four A.M. on the 21st, another heavy mass coming violently in contact with the bergs and cables, threatened to sweep away every remaining security. Our situation, with this additional strain, the mass which had disturbed us fixing itself upon the weather-cable, and an increasing wind and swell setting considerably on the shore, became more and more precarious; and indeed, under circumstances as critical as can well be imagined, nothing but the urgency and importance of the object we had in view—that of saving the *Fury* if she was to be saved—could have prevented my making sail, and keeping the *Hecla* under way till matters mended. More hawsers were run out, however, and enabled us still to hold on; and after six hours of disturbed rest, all hands were again set to work to get the *Fury's* anchors, cables, rudder, and spars on board, these things being absolutely necessary for her equipment, should we be able to get her out. At two P.M. the crews were called on board to dinner, which they had not finished when several not very large masses p. 80of ice drove along the shore near us at a quick rate, and two or three successively coming in violent contact either with the *Hecla* or the bergs to which she was attached, convinced me that very little additional pressure would tear everything away, and drive both ships on shore. I saw that the moment had arrived when the *Hecla* could no longer be kept in her present situation with the smallest chance of safety, and therefore immediately got under sail, dispatching Captain Hoppner with every individual, except a few for working the ship, to continue getting the things on board the *Fury*, while the *Hecla* stood off and on. It was a quarter-past three P.M. when we cast off, the wind then blowing fresh from the north-east, or about two points upon the land, which caused some surf on the beach. Captain Hoppner had scarcely been an hour on board the *Fury*, and was busily engaged in getting the anchors and cables on board, when we observed some large pieces of not very heavy ice closing in with the land near her; and at twenty minutes past four P.M., being an hour and five minutes after the *Hecla* had cast off, I was informed by signal that the *Fury* was on shore. Making a tack in-shore, but not being able, even under a press of canvas, to get very near her, owing to a strong southerly current which prevailed within a mile or two of the land, I perceived that she had been apparently driven up the beach by two or three of the grounded masses forcing her onwards before them, and these, as well as the ship, seemed now so firmly aground as entirely to block her in on the seaward side. As the navigating of the *Hecla* with only ten men on board required constant attention and care, I could not at this time with propriety leave the ship to go on board the *Fury*. This, however, I the less regretted as Captain p. 81Hoppner was thoroughly acquainted with all my views and intentions, and I felt confident that, under his direction, nothing would be left undone to endeavour to save the ship. I, therefore, directed him by telegraph, "if he thought nothing could be done at present, to return on board with all hands until the wind changed;" for this alone, as far as I could see the state of the *Fury*, seemed to offer the smallest chance of clearing the shore, so as to enable us to proceed with our work, or to attempt hauling the ship off the ground. About seven P.M. Captain Hoppner returned to the *Hecla*, accompanied by all hands, except an officer with a party at the pumps, reporting to me that the *Fury* had been forced aground by the ice pressing on the masses lying near her, and bringing home, if not breaking, the seaward anchor, so that the ship was soon found to have sewed from two to three feet fore and aft.

With the ship thus situated, and masses of heavy ice constantly coming in, it was Captain Hoppner's decided opinion, as well as that of Lieutenants Austin and Ross, that to have laid out another anchor to seaward would have only been to expose it to the same damage as there was reason to suppose had been incurred with the other, without the most distant hope of doing any service; especially as the ship had been driven on shore, by a most unfortunate coincidence, just as the tide was beginning to fall. Indeed, in the present state of the *Fury*, nothing short of chopping and sawing up a part of the ice under her stern could by any possibility have effected her release, even if she had been already afloat. Under such circumstances, hopeless as for the time every seaman will admit them to have been, Captain Hoppner judiciously determined to return for the present, as directed by my p. 82telegraphic communication; but being anxious to keep the ship free from water as long as possible, he left an officer and a small party of men to continue working at the pumps so long as a communication could be kept up between the *Hecla* and the shore. Every moment, however, decreased the practicability of doing this; and finding, soon after Captain Hoppner's return, that the current swept the *Hecla* a long way to the southward while hoisting up the boats, and that more ice was drifting in towards the shore, I was under the painful necessity of recalling the party at the pumps, rather than incur the risk, now an inevitable one, of parting company with them altogether. Accordingly Mr. Bird, with the last of the people, came on board at eight o'clock in the evening, having left eighteen inches of water in the well, and four pumps being requisite to keep her free. In three hours after Mr. Bird's return, more than half a mile of closely-packed ice intervened between the *Fury* and the open water in which we were beating, and before the morning this barrier had increased to four or five miles in breadth.

We carried a press of canvas all night, with a fresh breeze from the north, to enable us to keep abreast of the *Fury*, which, on account of the strong southerly current, we could only do by beating at some distance from the land. The breadth of the ice in-shore continued increasing during the day, but we could see no end to the water in which we were beating, either to the southward or eastward. Advantage was taken of the little leisure now allowed us, to let the people mend and wash their clothes, which they had scarcely had a moment to do for the last three weeks. We also completed the thrumming of a second sail for putting under the *Fury's* keel whenever we should be enabled to haul her off the shore. It fell p. 83quite calm in the evening, when the breadth of the ice in-shore had increased to six or seven miles. We did not during the day perceive any current setting to the southward, but in the course of the night we were drifted four or five leagues to the south-westward, in which situation we had a distinct view of a large extent of land, which had before been seen for the first time by some of our gentlemen who walked from where the *Fury* lay. This land trends very much to the westward, a little beyond the Fury Point, the name by which I have distinguished that headland near which we had attempted to heave the *Fury* down, and which is very near the southern part of this coast, seen in the year 1819. It then sweeps round into a large bay, formed by a long, low beach several miles in extent, afterwards joining higher land, and running in a south-easterly direction to a point which terminated our view of it in that quarter, and which bore from us S. 580 W. distant six or seven leagues. This headland I named Cape Garry, after my worthy friend Nicholas Garry, Esq., one of the most active members of the Hudson's Bay Company, and a gentleman most warmly interested in everything connected with northern discovery. The whole of the bay (which I named after my much esteemed friend, Francis Cresswell, Esq.), as well as the land to the southward, was free from ice for several miles, and to the southward and eastward scarcely any was to be seen, while a dark water-sky indicated a perfectly navigable sea in that direction; but between us and the Fury there was a compact body of ice eight or nine miles in breadth. Had we now been at liberty to take advantage of the favourable prospect before us, I have little doubt we should without much difficulty have made considerable progress.

p. 84A southerly breeze enabling us to regain our northing, we ran along the margin of the ice, but were led so much to the eastward by it, that we could approach the ship no nearer than before during the whole day. She appeared to us at this distance to have a much greater heel than when the people left her, which made us still more anxious to get near her. A south-west wind gave us hopes of the ice setting off from the land, but it produced no good effect during the whole of the 24th. We, therefore, beat again to the southward to see if we could manage to get in with the land anywhere about the shores of the bay; but this was now impracticable, the ice being once more closely packed there. We could only wait, therefore, in patience, for some alteration in our favour. The latitude at noon was 720 34' 57", making our distance from the *Fury* twelve miles, which by the morning of the 25th had increased to at least five leagues, the ice continuing to "pack" between us and the shore. The wind, however, now gradually drew round to the westward, giving us hopes of a change, and we continued to ply about the margin of the ice, in constant readiness for taking advantage of any opening that might occur. It favoured us so much by streaming off in the course of the day, that by seven P.M. we had nearly reached a channel of clear water, which kept open for seven or eight miles from the land. Being impatient to obtain a sight of the *Fury*, and the wind becoming light, Captain Hoppner and myself left the *Hecla* in two boats, and reached the ship at half-past nine, or about three-quarters of an hour before high water, being the most favourable time of tide for arriving to examine her condition.

We found her heeling so much outward, that her main channels were within a foot of the water; and the large p. 85floe-piece, which was still alongside of her, seemed alone to support her below water, and to prevent her falling over still more considerably. The ship had been forced much further up the beach than before, and she had now in her bilge above nine feet of water, which reached higher than the lower-deck beams. On looking down the stern-post, which, seen against the light-coloured ground, and in shoal water, was now very distinctly visible, we found that she had pushed the stones at the bottom up before her, and that the broken keel, sternpost, and deadwood had, by the recent pressure, been more damaged and turned up than before. She appeared principally to hang upon the ground abreast of the gangway, where, at high water, the depth was eleven feet alongside her keel; forward and aft from thirteen to sixteen feet; so that at low tide, allowing the usual fall of five or six feet, she would be lying in a depth of from five to ten feet only. The first hour's inspection of the *Fury's* condition too plainly assured me that exposed as she was, and forcibly pressed up upon an open and stony beach, her holds full of water, and the damage of her hull to all appearance and in all probability more considerable than before, without any adequate means of hauling her off to seaward, or securing her from the further incursions of the ice, every endeavour of ours to get her off, or if got off, to float her to any known place of safety, would be at once utterly hopeless in itself, and productive of extreme risk to our remaining ship.

Being anxious, however, in a case of so much importance, to avail myself of the judgment and experience of others, I directed Captain Hoppner, in conjunction with Lieutenants Austin and Sherer, and Mr. Pulfer, carpenter, being the officers who accompanied me to the *Fury*, to p. 86hold a survey upon her, and to report their opinions to me. And to prevent the possibility of the officers receiving any bias from my own opinion, the order was given to them the moment we arrived on board the *Fury*.

Captain Hoppner and the other officers, after spending several hours in attentively examining every part of the ship, both within and without, and maturely weighing all the circumstances of her situation, gave it as their opinion that it would be quite impracticable to make her seaworthy, even if she could be hauled off, which would first require the water to be got out of the ship, and the holds to be once more entirely cleared. Mr. Pulfer, the carpenter of the *Fury*, considered that it would occupy five days to clear the ship of water; that if she were got off, all the pumps would not be sufficient to keep her free, in consequence of the additional damage she seemed to have sustained; and that, if even hove down, twenty days' work, with the means we possessed, would be required for making her seaworthy. Captain Hoppner and the other officers were, therefore, of opinion that an absolute necessity existed for abandoning the *Fury*. My own opinion being thus confirmed as to the utter hopelessness of saving her, and feeling more strongly than ever the responsibility which attached to me of preserving the *Hecla* unhurt, it was with extreme pain and regret that I made the signal for the *Fury's* officers and men to be sent for their clothes, most of which had been put on shore with the stores.

The *Hecla's* bower-anchor, which had been placed on the beach, was sent on board as soon as the people came on shore; but her remaining cable was too much entangled with the grounded ice to be disengaged without great loss of time. Having allowed the officers and men p. 87an hour for packing up their clothes, and what else belonging to them the water in the ship had not covered, the *Fury's* boats were hauled up on the beach, and at two A.M. I left her, and was followed by Captain Hoppner, Lieutenant Austin, and the last of the people in half an hour after.

The whole of the *Fury's* stores were of necessity left either on board her or on shore, every spare corner that we could find in the *Hecla* being now absolutely required for the accommodation of our double complement of officers and men, whose cleanliness and health could only be maintained by keeping the decks as clear and well ventilated as our limited space would permit. The spot where the *Fury* was left is in latitude 720 42' 30", the longitude by chronometers is 910 50' 05", the dip of the magnetic needle 880 19' 22", and the variation 1290 25' westerly.

When the accident first happened to the *Fury*, I confidently expected to have been able to repair her damages in good time to take advantage of a large remaining part of the navigable season in the prosecution of the voyage; and while the clearing of the ship was going on with so much alacrity, and the repairs seemed to be within the reach of our means and resources, I still flattered myself with the same hope. But as soon as the gales began to destroy, with a rapidity of which we had before no conception, our sole defence from the incursions of the ice, as well as the only trustworthy means we before possessed of holding the *Hecla* out for heaving the *Fury* down, I confess that the prospect of the necessity then likely to arise for removing her to some other station, was sufficient to shake every reasonable expectation I had hitherto cherished of the ultimate accomplishment of our object. Those p. 88expectations were now at an end. With a twelvemonth's provisions for both ships' companies, extending our resources only to the autumn of the following year, it would have been folly to hope for final success, considering the small progress we had already made, the uncertain nature of this navigation, and the advanced period of the present season. I was, therefore, reduced to the only remaining conclusion that it was my duty, under all the circumstances of the case, to return to England, in compliance with the plain tenor of my instructions. As soon as the boats were hoisted up, therefore, and the anchor stowed, the ship's head was put to the north-eastward, with a light air off the land, in order to gain an offing before the ice should again set inshore.

CHAPTER VII.

Some Remarks upon the loss of the Fury — And on the Natural History, &c., of the Coast of North Somerset — Arrive at Neill's Harbour — Death of John Page — Leave Neill's Harbour — Recross the Ice in Baffin's Bay — Heavy Gales — Aurora Borealis — Temperature of the Sea — Arrival in England.

The accident which had now befallen the *Fury*, and which, when its fatal result was finally ascertained, at once put an end to every prospect of success in the main object of this voyage, is not an event which will excite surprise in the minds of those who are either personally acquainted with the true nature of this precarious navigation, or have had patience to follow me through the tedious and monotonous detail of our operations during seven successive summers. To any persons thus qualified to judge it will be plain that an occurrence of this nature was at all times rather to be expected than otherwise, p. 89and that the only real cause for wonder has been our long exemption from such a catastrophe. I can confidently affirm, and I trust that on such an occasion I may be permitted to make the remark, that the mere safety of the ships has never been more than a secondary object in the conduct of the expeditions under my command. To push forward while there was any open water to enable us to do so has uniformly been our first endeavour; it has not been until the channel has actually terminated that we have ever been accustomed to look for a place of shelter, to which the ships were then conducted with all possible despatch; and I may safely venture to predict that no ship acting otherwise will ever accomplish the Northwest Passage. On numerous occasions, which will easily recur to the memory of those I have had the honour to command, the ships might easily have been placed among the ice and left to drift with it in comparative, if not absolute, security, when the holding them on has been preferred, though attended with hourly and imminent peril. This was precisely the case on the present occasion; the ships might certainly have been pushed into the ice a day or two, or even a week beforehand, and thus preserved from all risk of being forced on shore; but where they would have been drifted, and when they would have been again disengaged from the ice, or at liberty to take advantage of the occasional openings in-shore (by which alone the navigation of these seas is to be performed with any degree of certainty), I believe it impossible for any one to form the most distant idea. Such, then, being the necessity for constant and unavoidable risk, it cannot reasonably excite surprise that on a single occasion out of so many in which the same accident seemed, as it were, impending, it should actually have taken place.

p. 90The ice we met with after leaving Port Bowen, previously to the *Fury's* disaster, and for some days after, I consider to have been much the lightest as well as the most broken we have ever had to contend with. During the time we were shut up at our last station near the *Fury*, one or two floes of very large dimensions drifted past us; and these were of that heavy "hummocky" kind which we saw off Cape Kater in the beginning of August, 1819. On the whole, however, Mr. Allison and myself had constant occasion to remark the total absence of floes, and the unusual lightness of the other ice. We thought, indeed, that this latter circumstance might account for its being almost incessantly in motion on this coast; for heavy ice, when once it is pressed home upon the shore, and has ceased to move, generally remains quiet, until a change of wind or tide makes it slacken. But with lighter ice, the frequent breaking and doubling of the parts which sustain the strain, whenever any increase of pressure takes place, will set the whole body once more in motion till the space is again filled up. This was so often the case while our ships lay in the most exposed situations on this unsheltered coast, that we were never relieved for a moment from the apprehension of some new and increased pressure.

The summer of 1825 was, beyond all doubt, the warmest and most favourable we had experienced since that of 1818. Not more than two or three days occurred, during the months of July and August, in which that heavy fall of snow took place which so commonly converts the aspect of Nature in these regions, in a single hour, from the cheerfulness of summer into the dreariness of winter. Indeed, we experienced very little either of snow, rain, or fog; vegetation, wherever the soil allowed any to spring p. 91up, was extremely luxuriant and forward; a great deal of the old snow which had laid on the ground during the last season was rapidly dissolving even early in August; and every appearance of Nature exhibited a striking contrast with the last summer, while it seemed evidently to furnish an extraordinary compensation for its rigour and inclemency.

We have scarcely ever visited a coast on which so little of animal life occurs. For days together, only one or two seals, a single seahorse, and now and then a flock of ducks, were seen. I have already mentioned, however, as an exception to this scarcity of animals, the numberless kittiwakes which were flying about the remarkable spout of water; and we were one day visited, at the place where the *Fury* was left, by hundreds of white whales sporting about in the shoal water close to the beach. No black whales were ever seen on this coast. Two reindeer were observed by the gentlemen who extended their walks inland; but this was the only summer in which we did not procure a single pound of venison. Indeed, the whole of our supplies obtained in this way during the voyage, including fish, flesh, and fowl, did not exceed twenty pounds per man.

During the time that we were made fast upon this coast, in which situation alone observations on current can be satisfactorily made, it is certain that the ice was setting to the southward, and sometimes at a rapid rate, full seven days out of every ten on an average. Had I now witnessed this for the first time in these seas, I should probably have concluded that there was a constant southerly set at this season; but the experience we had before obtained of that superficial current which every breeze of wind creates in a sea encumbered with ice, p. 92coupled with the fact that while this set was noticed we had an almost continual prevalence of northerly winds, inclines me to believe that it was to be attributed—chiefly at least—to this circumstance, especially as, on one or two occasions, with rather a light breeze from the southward, the ice did set slowly in the opposite direction. It is not by a few unconnected observations that a question of this kind is to be settled, as the facts noticed during our detention near the west end of Melville Island in 1820 will abundantly testify; every light air of wind producing, in half an hour's time, an extraordinary change of current setting at an incredible rate along the land.

The existence of these variable and irregular currents adds, of course, very much to the difficulty of determining the true direction of the flood-tide, the latter being generally much the weaker of the two, and therefore either wholly counteracted by the current, or simply tending to accelerate it. On this account, though I attended very carefully to the subject of the tides, I cannot pretend to say for certain from what direction the flood-tide comes on this coast; the impression on my mind, however, has been, upon the whole, in favour of its flowing from the southward. The time of high water on the full and change days of the moon is from half-past eleven to twelve o'clock, being nearly the same as at Port Bowen; but the tides are so irregular at times, that in the space of three days the retardation will occasionally not amount to an hour. I observed, however, that, as the days of full and change, or of the moon's quarter approached, the irregularity was corrected, and the time rectified, by some tide of extraordinary duration. The mean rise and fall was about six feet.

p. 93The weather continuing nearly calm during the 26th, and the ice keeping at the distance of several miles from the land, gave us an opportunity of clearing our decks, and stowing the things belonging to the *Fury's* crew more comfortably for their accommodation and convenience. I now felt more sensibly than ever the necessity I have elsewhere pointed out, of both ships employed on this kind of service being of the same size, equipped in the same manner, and alike efficient in every respect. The way in which we had been able to apply every article for assisting to heave the *Fury* down, without the smallest doubt or selection as to size or strength, proved an excellent practical example of the value of being thus able, at a moment's warning, to double the means and resources of either ship in case of necessity. In fact, by this arrangement, nothing but a harbour to secure the ships was wanted, to have completed the whole operation in as effectual a manner as in a dockyard; for not a shore, or outrigger, or any other precaution was omitted, that is usually attended to on such occasions, and all as good and effective as could anywhere have been desired. The advantages were now scarcely less conspicuous in the accommodation of the officers and men, who in a short time became little less comfortable than in their own ship; whereas, in a smaller vessel, comfort, to say nothing of health, would have been quite out of the question. Having thus experienced the incalculable benefit of the establishment composing this expedition, I am anxious to repeat my conviction of the advantages that will always be found to attend it in the equipment of any two ships intended for discovery.

A little snow, which had fallen in the course of the last two or three days, now remained upon the land, p. 94lightly powdering the higher parts, especially those having a northern aspect, and creating a much more wintry sensation than the large broad patches or drifts, which, on all tolerably high land in these regions, remain undissolved during the whole of each successive summer. With the exception of a few such patches here and there, the whole of this coast was now free from snow before the middle of August.

A breeze from the northward freshening up strong on the 27th, we stretched over to the eastern shore of Prince Regent's Inlet, and this with scarcely any obstruction from ice. We could, indeed, scarcely believe this the same sea which, but a few weeks before, had been loaded with one impenetrable body of closely packed ice from shore to shore, and as far as the eye could discern to the southward. We found this land rather more covered with the newly fallen snow than that to the westward; but there was no ice, except the grounded masses, anywhere along the shore. Having a great deal of heavy work to do in the re-stowage of the holds which could not well be accomplished at sea, and also a quantity of water to fill for our increased complement, I determined to take advantage of our fetching the entrance of Neill's Harbour to put in here, in order to prepare the ship completely for crossing the Atlantic. I was desirous also of ascertaining the depth of water in this place, which was wanting to complete Lieutenant Sherer's survey of it. At one P.M., therefore, after communicating to the officers and ships' companies my intention to return to England, I left the ship, accompanied by Lieutenant Sherer in a second boat, to obtain the necessary soundings for conducting the ship to the anchorage, and to lay down a buoy in the proper berth. Finding the harbour an p. 95extremely convenient one for our purpose, we worked the ship in, and at four P.M. anchored in thirteen fathoms, but afterwards shifted out to eighteen on a bottom of soft mud. Almost at the moment of our dropping the anchor, John Page, seaman of the *Fury*, departed this life; he had for several months been affected with a scrofulous disorder, and had been gradually sinking for some time.

The funeral of the deceased took place after Divine service had been performed on the 28th; the body being followed to the grave by a procession of all the officers, seamen, and marines of both ships, and every solemnity observed which the occasion demanded. The grave is situated near the beach close to the anchorage, and a board was placed at the head as a substitute for a tombstone, having on it a copper-plate with the usual inscription.

This duty being performed, we immediately commenced landing the casks and filling water; but notwithstanding the large streams which, a short time before, had been running into the harbour, we could hardly obtain enough for our purpose by sinking a cask with holes in it. I have no doubt that this rapid dissolution of all the snow on land so high as this, was the result of an unusually warm summer. This work, together with the entire re-stowage of all the holds, occupied the whole of the 29th and 30th; during which time Lieutenant Sherer was employed in completing the survey of the harbour, more especially the soundings, which the presence of ice had before prevented. These arrangements had just been completed when the north-easterly wind died away, and was succeeded on the morning of the 31st by a light air from the north-west. As soon as we had sent to ascertain p. 96that the sea was clear of ice on the outside, and that the breeze which blew in the harbour was the true one, we weighed and stood out, and before noon had cleared the shoals at the entrance.

Neill's Harbour, the only one on this eastern coast of Prince Regent's Inlet, except Port Bowen, to which it is far superior, corresponds with one of the apparent openings seen at a distance in 1819, and marked on the chart of that voyage as a "valley or bay." We found it not merely a convenient place of shelter but a most excellent harbour, with sufficient space for a great number of ships, and holding-ground of the best quality, consisting of a tenacious mud of a greenish colour, in which the flukes of an anchor are entirely embedded. A great deal of the anchoring ground is entirely landlocked, and some shoal points which narrow the entrance would serve to break off any heavy sea from the eastward. The depth of water in most parts is greater than could be wished, but several good berths are pointed out in the accompanying survey made by Lieutenant Sherer. The beach on the west side is a fine bold one, with four fathoms within twenty yards of low water mark, and consists of small pebbles of limestone. The formation of the rocks about the harbour is so similar to that of Port Bowen that no description of them is necessary. The harbour may best be known by its latitude; by the very remarkable flat-topped hill eight miles south of it, which I have named after Lieutenant Sherer who observed its latitude; by the high cliffs on the south side of the entrance, and the comparative low land on the north. The high land is the more peculiar, as consisting of that very regular horizontal stratification appearing to be supported by buttresses, which characterises a large portion of the p. 97western shore of Prince Regent's Inlet, but is not seen on any part of this coast so well marked as here. It is a remarkable circumstance, and such as, I believe, very rarely occurs, that from the point of this land forming the entrance of the harbour to the southward, and where the cliffs rise at once to a perpendicular height of not less than five or six hundred feet, a shoal stretches off to the distance of one-third of a mile, having from three to eight fathoms upon it. I have reason to think indeed that there is not more than from ten to fourteen fathoms anywhere across between this and the low point on the other side, thus forming a sort of bar, though the depth of water is much more than sufficient for any ship to pass over. The latitude of Neill's Harbour is 730 09' 08"; the longitude by chronometers 890 01' 20".8; the dip of the magnetic needle 880 08'.25, and the variation 1180 48' westerly.

I have been thus particular in describing Neill's Harbour, because I am of opinion that at no very distant period the whalers may find it of service. The western coast of Baffin's Bay, now an abundant fishery, will probably, like most others, fail in a few years; for the whales will always in the course of time leave a place where they continue year after year to be molested. In that case, Prince Regent's Inlet will undoubtedly become a rendezvous for our ships, as well on account of the numerous fish there, as the facility with which any ship, having once crossed the ice in Baffin's Bay, is sure to reach it during the months of July and August. We saw nine or ten black whales the evening of our arrival in Neill's Harbour; these, like most observed hereabouts, and I believe on the western coast of Baffin's Bay generally, were somewhat below the middle size.

p. 98Finding the wind at north-west in Prince Regent's Inlet, we were barely able to lie along the eastern coast. As the breeze freshened in the course of the day, a great deal of loose ice in extensive streams and patches came drifting down from the Leopold Islands, occasioning us some trouble in picking our way to the northward. By carrying a press of sail, however, we were enabled, towards night, to get into clearer water, and by four A.M. on the 1st of September, having beat to windward of a compact body of ice which had fixed itself on the lee shore about Cape York, we soon came into a perfectly open sea in Barrow's Strait, and were enabled to bear away to the eastward. We now considered ourselves fortunate in having got out of harbour when we did, as the ice would probably have filled up every inlet on that shore in a few hours after we left it.

The wind heading us from the eastward on the 2nd, with fog and wet weather, obliged us to stretch across the Sound, in doing which we had occasion to remark the more than usual number of icebergs that occurred in this place, which was abreast of Navy Board Inlet. Many of these were large and of the long flat kind, which appear to me to be peculiar to the western coast of Baffin's Bay. I have no doubt that this more than usual quantity of icebergs in Sir James Lancaster's Sound was to be attributed to the extraordinary prevalence and strength of the easterly winds during this summer, which would drive them from the eastern parts of Baffin's Bay. They now occurred in the proportion of at least four for one that we had ever before observed here.

Being again favoured with a fair wind, we now stretched to the eastward, still in an open sea; and our curiosity was particularly excited to see the present p. 99situation of the ice in the middle of Baffin's Bay, and to compare it with that in 1824. This comparison we were enabled to make the more fairly, because the season at which we might expect to come to it coincided, within three or four days, with that in which we left it the preceding year. The temperature of the sea-water now increased to 380, soon after leaving the Sound, where it had generally been from 330 to 350, whereas at the same season last year it rose no higher than 320 anywhere in the neighbourhood, and remained even so high as that only for a very short time. This circumstance seemed to indicate the total absence of ice from those parts of the sea which had last autumn been wholly covered by it. Accordingly, on the 5th, being thirty miles beyond the spot in which we had before contended with numerous difficulties from ice, not a piece was to be seen, except one or two solitary bergs; and it was not till the following day, in latitude 720 45', and longitude 640 44', or about one hundred and twenty-seven miles to the eastward of where we made our escape on the 9th of September, 1824, that we fell in with a body of ice so loose and open as scarcely to oblige us to alter our course for it. At three P.M. on the 7th, being in latitude 720 30', and longitude 600 05', and having, in the course of eighty miles that we had run through it, only made a single tack, we came to the margin of the ice, and got into an open sea on its eastern side. In the whole course of this distance the ice was so much spread, that it would not, if at all closely "packed," have occupied one-third of the same space. There were at this time thirty-nine bergs in sight, and some of them certainly not less than two hundred feet in height.

The narrowness and openness of the ice at this season, p. 100between the parallels of 730 and 740, when compared with its extent and closeness about the same time the preceding year, was a decided confirmation, if any were wanting, that the summer of 1824 was extremely unfavourable for penetrating to the westward about the usual latitudes. How it had proved elsewhere we could not of course conjecture, till, on the 8th, being in latitude 710 55', longitude

600 30', and close to the margin of the ice, we fell in with the *Alfred,* *Ellison,* and *Elizabeth,* whalers of Hull, all running to the northward, even at this season, to look for whales. From them we learned that the *Ellison* was one of the two ships we saw, when beset in the "pack" on the 18th July, 1824; and that they were then, as we had conjectured, on their return from the northward, in consequence of having failed in effecting a passage to the westward. The master of the *Ellison* informed us that, after continuing their course along the margin of the ice to the southward, they at length passed through it to the western land without any difficulty, in the latitude of 680 to 690. Many other ships had also crossed about the same parallels, even in three or four days; but none, it seemed, had succeeded in doing so, as usual, to the northward. Thus it plainly appeared (and I need not hesitate to confess that to me the information was satisfactory) that our bad success in pushing across the ice in Baffin's Bay in 1824, had been caused by circumstances neither to be foreseen nor controlled; namely, by a particular position of the ice, which, according to the best information I have been able to collect, has never before occurred during the only six years that it has been customary for the whalers to cross this ice at all, and which, therefore, in all probability, will seldom occur again.

p. 101If we seek for a cause for the ice thus hanging with more than ordinary tenacity to the northward, the comparative coldness of the season indicated by our meteorological observations may perhaps be considered sufficient to furnish it. For as the annual clearing of the northern parts of Baffin's Bay depends entirely on the time of the disruption of the ice, and the rate at which it is afterwards drifted to the southward by the excess of northerly winds, any circumstance tending to retain it in the bays and inlets to a later period than usual, and subsequently to hold it together in large floes, which drive more slowly than smaller masses, would undoubtedly produce the effect in question. There is, at all events, one useful practical inference to be drawn from what has been stated, which is that, though perhaps in a considerable majority of years a northern latitude may prove the most favourable for crossing in, yet seasons will sometimes intervene in which it will be a matter of great uncertainty whereabouts to make the attempt with the best hope of success.

As the whaling ships were not homeward bound, having as yet had indifferent success in the fishery, I did not consider it necessary to send despatches by them. After an hour's communication with them, and obtaining such information of a public nature as could not fail to be highly interesting to us, we made sail to the southward: while we observed them lying-to for some time after, probably to consult respecting the unwelcome information with which we had furnished them as to the whales, not one of which, by some extraordinary chance, we had seen since leaving Neill's Harbour. As this circumstance was entirely new to us, it seems not unlikely that the whales are already beginning to shift their ground, in p. 102consequence of the increased attacks which have been made upon them of late years in that neighbourhood.

On the 10th we had an easterly wind, which, gradually freshening to a gale, drew up the Strait from the southward, and blew strong for twenty-four hours from that quarter. In the course of the night, and while lying-to under the storm-sails, an iceberg was discovered, by its white appearance, under our lee. The main-topsail being thrown aback we were enabled to drop clear of this immense body, which would have been a dangerous neighbour in a heavy seaway. The wind moderated on the 11th, but on the following day another gale came on, which for nine or ten hours blew in most tremendous gusts from the same quarter, and raised a heavy sea. We happily came near no ice during the night, or it would scarcely have been possible to keep the ship clear of it. It abated after daylight on the 13th, but continued to blow an ordinary gale for twelve hours longer. It was remarkable that the weather was extremely clear overhead during the whole of this last gale, which is very unusual here with a southerly wind. Being favoured with a northerly breeze on the 15th we began to make some way to the southward. From nine A.M. to one P.M. a change of temperature in the sea water took place from 370 to 330. This circumstance seemed to indicate our approach to some ice projecting to the eastward beyond the straight and regular margin of the "pack," which was at this time not in sight. The indication proved correct and useful; for after passing several loose pieces of ice during the night, on the morning of the 15th, just at daybreak, we came to a considerable body of it, through which we continued to run to the southward. We were now in latitude 680 56', and in longitude 580 27', in which p. 103situation a great many bergs were in sight, and apparently aground. We ran through this ice, which was very heavy, but loose and much broken up, the whole day; when having sailed fifty-three miles S.S.E., and appearances being the same as ever, we hauled to the E.S.E., to endeavour to get clear before dark, which we were just enabled to effect after a run of thirty miles in that direction, and then bore up to the southward. After this we saw but one iceberg and one heavy loose piece previous to our clearing Davis's Strait.

On the 17th at noon we had passed to the southward of the Arctic Circle, and from this latitude to that of about 580 we had favourable winds and weather; but we remarked on this, as on several other occasions during this season, that a northerly breeze, contrary to ordinary observation, brought more moisture with it than any other. In the course of this run we also observed more drift-wood than we had ever done before, which I thought might possibly be owing to the very great prevalence of easterly winds this season driving it further from the coast of Greenland than usual. We saw very large flocks of kittiwakes, some of the whales called finners, and, as we supposed, a few also of the black kind, together with multitudes of porpoises.

On the morning of the 24th, notwithstanding the continuance of a favourable breeze, we met, in the latitude of 58=0, so heavy a swell from the north-eastward as to make the ship labour violently for four-and-twenty hours. The northerly wind then dying away was succeeded by a light air from the eastward with constant rain. A calm then followed for several hours, causing the ship to roll heavily in the hollow of the sea. On the morning of the 25th we had again an easterly wind, p. 104which in a few hours reduced us to the close-reefed topsails and reefed courses. At eight P.M. it freshened to a gale, which brought us under the main-topsail and storm-staysails, and at seven the following morning it increased to a gale of such violence from N.E.b.N. as does not very often occur at sea in these latitudes. The gusts were at times so tremendous as to set the sea quite in a foam, and threatened to tear the sails out of the bolt-ropes. It abated a little for four hours in the evening, but from nine P.M. till two the following morning blew with as great violence as before, with a high sea, and very heavy rain; constituting altogether as inclement weather as can well be conceived for about eighteen hours. The wind gradually drew to the westward, with dry weather, after the gale began to abate, and at six A.M. we were enabled to bear up and run to the eastward with a strong gale at north-west.

The indications of the barometer previous to and during this gale deserve to be noticed, because it is only about Cape Farewell that, in coming from the northward down Davis's Strait, this instrument begins to speak a language which has ever been intelligible to us as a weather-glass. As it is also certain that a "stormy spirit" resides in the neighbourhood of this headland, no less than in that of more famed ones to the south, it may become a matter of no small practical utility for ships passing it, especially in the autumn, to attend to the oscillations of the mercurial column. It is with this impression alone that I have detailed the otherwise uninteresting circumstances of the inclement weather we now experienced here; and which was accompanied by the following indications of the barometer. On the 24th, notwithstanding the change of wind from north to east, p. 105the mercury rose from 29.51 on that morning, to 29.72 at three A.M. the following day, but fell to 29.39 by nine P.M., with the strong but not violent breeze then blowing. After this it continued to descend very gradually, and had reached 28.84, which was its minimum, at three P.M. on the 26th, after which it continued to blow tremendously hard for eleven or twelve hours, the mercury uniformly though slowly ascending to 28.95 during that interval, and afterwards to 29.73 as the weather became moderate and fine in the course of the three following days.

After this gale the atmosphere seemed to be quite cleared, and we enjoyed a week of such remarkably fine weather as seldom occurs at this season of the year. We had then a succession of strong southerly winds, but were enabled to continue our progress to the eastward, so as to make Mould Head, towards the north-west end of the Orkney Islands, at daylight on the 10th of October; and the wind becoming more westerly we rounded North Ronaldsha Island at noon, and then shaped a course for Buchaness.

In running down Davis's Strait, as well as in crossing the Atlantic, we saw on this passage as well as in all our former autumnal ones, a good deal of the Aurora Borealis. It first began to display itself on the 15th of September, about the latitude of 69=0, appearing in the (true) south-east quarter as a bright luminous patch five or six degrees above the horizon, almost stationary for two or three hours together, but frequently altering its intensity, and occasionally sending up vivid streamers towards the zenith. It appeared in the same manner on several subsequent nights in the south-west, west, and east quarters of the heavens; and on the 20th a bright arch of it passed across the zenith from S.E. to N.W., appearing to be very p. 106close to the ship, and affording so strong a light as to throw the shadow of objects on the deck. The next brilliant display, however, of this beautiful phenomenon which we now witnessed, and which far surpassed anything of the kind observed at Port Bowen, occurred on the night of the 24th of September, in latitude 58=0, longitude 44=0. It first appeared in a (true) east direction, in detached masses like luminous clouds of yellow or sulphur-coloured light, about three degrees above the horizon. When this appearance had continued for about an hour, it began at nine P.M. to spread upwards, and gradually extended itself into a narrow band of light passing through the zenith and again downwards to the western horizon. Soon after this the streams of light seemed no longer to emanate from the eastward, but from a fixed point about one degree above the horizon on a true west bearing. From this point, as from the narrow point of a funnel, streams of light, resembling brightly illuminated vapour or smoke, appeared to be incessantly issuing, increasing in breadth as they proceeded, and darting with inconceivable velocity, such as the eye could scarcely keep pace with, upwards towards the zenith, and in the same easterly direction which the former arch had taken. The sky immediately under the spot from which the light issued appeared, by a deception very common in this phenomenon, to be covered with a dark cloud, whose outline the imagination might at times convert into that of the summit of a mountain, from which the light proceeded like the flames of a volcano. The streams of light as they were projected upwards did not consist of continuous vertical columns or streamers, but almost entirely of separate, though constantly renewed masses, which seemed to roll themselves p. 107laterally onward with a sort of undulating motion, constituting what I have understood to be meant by that modification of the Aurora called the "merry dancers," which is seen in beautiful perfection at the Shetland Islands. The general colour of the light was yellow, but an orange and a greenish tinge were at times very distinctly perceptible, the intensity of the light and colours being always the greatest when occupying the smallest space. Thus the lateral margins of the band or arch seemed at times to roll themselves inwards so as to approach each other, and in this case the light just at the edges became much more vivid than the rest. The intensity of light during the brightest part of the phenomenon, which continued three-quarters of an hour, could scarcely be inferior to that of the moon when full.

We once more remarked in crossing the Atlantic that the Aurora often gave a great deal of light at night, even when the sky was entirely overcast, and it was on that account impossible to say from what part of the heavens the light proceeded, though it was often fully equal to that afforded by the moon in her quarters. This was rendered particularly striking on the night of the 5th of October, in consequence of the frequent and almost instantaneous changes which took place in this way, the weather being rather dark and gloomy, but the sky at times so brightly illuminated, almost in an instant, as to give quite as much light as the full moon similarly clouded, and enabling one distinctly to recognise persons from one end of the ship to the other. We did not on any one occasion perceive the compasses to be affected by the Aurora Borealis.

As we approached the Orkneys, I demanded from the officers, in compliance with my instructions from my p. 108Lords Commissioners of the Admiralty, all the logs, journals, drawings, and charts, which had been made during the voyage. After rounding the north end of the Orkneys on the 10th of October, we were on the 12th met by a strong southerly wind when off Peterhead. I, therefore, immediately landed (for the second time) at that place; and, setting off without delay for London, arrived at the Admiralty on the 16th.

Notwithstanding the ill success which had attended our late efforts, it may in some degree be imagined what gratification I experienced at this time in seeing the whole of the *Hecla's* crew, and also those of the *Fury* (with the two exceptions already mentioned), return to their native country in as good health as when they left it eighteen months before. The *Hecla* arrived at Sheerness on the 20th of October, where she was detained for a few days for the purpose of Captain Hoppner, his officers, and ship's company, being put upon their trial (according to the customary and indispensable rule in such cases) for the loss of the *Fury*; when, it is scarcely necessary to add, they received an honourable acquittal. The *Hecla* then proceeded to Woolwich, and was paid off on the 21st of November.

p. 109ACCOUNT OF THE ESQUIMAUX OF MELVILLE PENINSULA AND THE ADJOINING ISLANDS,

More particularly of Winter Island and Igloolik.

The number of individuals composing the tribe of Esquimaux assembled at Winter Island and Igloolik was two hundred and nineteen, of whom sixty-nine were men, seventy-seven women, and seventy-three children. Two or three of the men, from their appearance and infirmities, as well as from the age of their children, must have been near seventy; the rest were from twenty to about fifty. The majority of the women were comparatively young, or from twenty to five-and-thirty, and three or four only seemed to have reached sixty. Of the children, about one-third were under four years old, and the rest from that age upwards to sixteen or seventeen. Out of one hundred and fifty-five individuals who passed the winter at Igloolik, we knew of eighteen deaths and of only nine births.

The stature of these people is much below that of Europeans in general. One man, who was unusually tall, measured five feet ten inches, and the shortest was only four feet eleven inches and a half. Of twenty individuals of each sex measured at Igloolik, the range was: —

Men. —From 5 ft. 10 in. to 4 ft. 11 in. The average height, 5 ft. 5⅓ in.

p. 110Women. —From 5 ft. 3= in. to 4 ft. 8> in. The average height, 5 ft. =in.

The women, however, generally appear shorter than they really are, both from the unwieldy nature of their clothes and from a habit, which they early acquire, of stooping considerably forward in order to balance the weight of the child they carry in their hood.

In their figure they are rather well-formed than otherwise. Their knees are indeed rather large in proportion, but their legs are straight, and the hands and feet, in both sexes, remarkably small. The younger individuals were all plump, but none of them corpulent; the women inclined the most to this last extreme, and their flesh was, even in the youngest individuals, quite loose and without firmness.

Their faces are generally round and full, eyes small and black, nose also small and sunk far in between the cheek bones, but not much flattened. It is remarkable that one man, *Tĕ-ă*, his brother, his wife, and two daughters had good Roman noses, and one of the latter was an extremely pretty young woman. Their teeth are short, thick, and close, generally regular, and in the young persons almost always white. The elderly women were still well furnished in this way, though their teeth were usually a good deal worn down, probably by the habit of chewing the seal-skins for making boots.

In the young of both sexes the complexion is clear and transparent, and the skin smooth. The colour of the latter, when divested of oil and dirt, is scarcely a shade darker than that of a deep brunette, so that the blood is plainly perceptible when it mounts into the cheeks. In the old folks, whose faces were much wrinkled, the skin appears of a much more dingy hue, the dirt being less p. 111easily, and therefore less frequently, dislodged from them. Besides the smallness of their eyes, there are two peculiarities in this feature common to almost all of them. The first consists in the eye not being horizontal as with us, but coming much lower at the end next the nose than at the other. Of the second an account by Mr. Edwards will be given in another place.

By whatever peculiarities, however, they may in general be distinguished, they are by no means ill-looking people; and there were among them three or four grown-up persons of each sex who, when divested of their skin-dresses, their tattooing, and, above all, of their dirt, might have been considered pleasing-looking, if not handsome, people in any town in Europe. This remark applies more generally to the children also; several of whom had complexions nearly as fair as that of Europeans, and whose little bright black eyes gave a fine expression to their countenances.

The hair both of males and females is black, glossy, and straight. The men usually wear it rather long, and allow it to hang about their heads in a loose and slovenly manner. A few of the younger men, and especially those who had been about the shores of the *Welcome*, had it cut straight upon the forehead, and two or three had a circular patch upon the crown of the head, where the hair was quite short and thin, somewhat after the manner of Capuchin friars. The women pride themselves extremely on the length and thickness of their hair; and it was not without reluctance on their part, and the same on that of their husbands, that they were induced to dispose of any of it. When inclined to be neat they separate their locks into two equal parts, one of which hangs on each side of their heads and in front of their shoulders. To p. 112stiffen and bind these they use a narrow strap of deerskin attached at one end to a round piece of bone, fourteen inches long, tapered to a point, and covered over with leather. This looks like a little whip, the handle of which is placed up and down the hair, and the strap wound round it in a number of spiral turns, making the tail thus equipped very much resemble one of those formerly worn by our seamen. The strap of this article of dress, which is altogether called a *tŏglēēgă*, is so made from the deerskin as to show, when bound round the hair, alternate turns of white and dark fur, which give it a very neat and ornamental appearance. On ordinary occasions it is considered slovenly not to have the hair thus dressed, and the neatest of the women never visited the ships without it. Those who are less nice dispose their hair into a loose plait on each side, or have one *tŏglēēgă* and one plait; and others again, wholly disregarding the business of the toilet, merely tucked their hair in under the breast of their jackets. Some of the women's hair was tolerably fine, but would not in this respect bear a comparison with that of an Englishwoman. In both sexes it is full of vermin, which they are in the constant habit of picking out and eating; a man and his wife will sit for an hour together performing for each other that friendly office. The women have a comb, which, however, seems more intended for ornament than use, as we seldom or never observed them comb their hair. When a woman's husband is ill she wears her hair loose, and cuts it off as a sign of mourning if he dies — a custom agreeing with that of the Greenlanders. It is probable also, from what has been before said, that some opprobrium is attached to the loss of a woman's hair when no such occasion demands this sacrifice. The men wear the hair on the upper lip and p. 113chin, from an inch to an inch and a half in length, and some were distinguished by a little tuft between the chin and lower lip.

The dresses both of male and female are composed almost entirely of deer-skin, in which respect they differ from those of most Esquimaux before met with. In the form of the dress they vary very little from those so repeatedly described. The jacket, which is close, but not tight, all round, comes as low as the hips, and has sleeves reaching to the wrist. In that of the women, the tail or flap behind is very broad, and so long as almost to touch the ground; while a shorter and narrower one before reaches half-way down the thigh. The men have also a tail in the hind part of their jacket, but of smaller dimensions; but before it is generally straight or ornamented by a single scollop. The hood of the jacket, which forms the only covering for their head, is much the largest in that of the women, for the purpose of holding a child. The back of the jacket also bulges out in the middle to give the child a footing, and a strap or girdle below this, and secured round the waist by two large wooden buttons in front, prevents the infant from falling through, when, the hood being in use, it is necessary thus to deposit it. The sleeves of the women's jackets are made more square and loose about the shoulders than those of the men, for the convenience, as we understood, of more readily depositing a child in the hood; and they have a habit of slipping their arms out of them, and keeping them in contact with their bodies for the sake of warmth, just as we do with our fingers in our gloves in very cold weather.

In winter every individual, when in the open air, wears two jackets, of which the outer one (*Cāppĕ-tēggă*) has the hair outside, and the inner one (*Attēēgă*) next the p. 114body. Immediately on entering the hut the men take off their outer jacket, beat the snow from it, and lay it by. The upper garment of the females, besides being cut according to a regular and uniform pattern, and sewed with exceeding neatness, which is the case with all the dresses of these people, has also the flaps ornamented in a very becoming manner by a neat border of deer-skin, so arranged as to display alternate breadths of white and dark fur. This is, moreover, usually beautified by a handsome fringe, consisting of innumerable long narrow threads of leather hanging down from it. This ornament is not uncommon also in the outer jackets of the men. When seal-hunting they fasten up the tails of their jackets with a button behind.

Their breeches, of which in winter they also wear two pairs, and similarly disposed as to the fur, reach below the knee, and fasten with a string drawn tight round the waist. Though these have little or no waist-band, and do not come very high, the depth of the jackets, which considerably overlap them, serves very effectually to complete the covering of the body.

Their legs and feet are so well clothed, that no degree of cold can well affect them. When a man goes on a sealing excursion he first puts on a pair of deer-skin boots (*Allĕktēēgă*) with the hair inside and reaching to the knee, where they tie. Over these come a pair of shoes of the same material; next a pair of dressed seal-skin boots perfectly water-tight; and over all a corresponding pair of shoes, tying round the instep. These last are made just like the moccasin of a North American Indian, being neatly crimped at the toes, and having several serpentine pieces of hide sewn across the sole to prevent wearing. The water-tight boots and shoes are made of p. 115the skin of the small seal (*neitiek*), except the soles, which consist of the skin of the large seal (*oguke*); this last is also used for their fishing-lines. When the men are not prepared to encounter wet they wear an outer boot of deer-skin with the hair outside.

The inner boot of the women, unlike that of the men, is loose round the leg, coming as high as the knee-joint behind, and in front carried up, by a long pointed flap, nearly to the waist, and there fastened to the breeches. The upper boot, with the hair as usual outside, corresponds with the other in shape, except that it is much more full, especially on the outer side, where it bulges out so preposterously as to give the women the most awkward, bow-legged appearance imaginable. This superfluity of boot has probably originated in the custom, still common among the native women of Labrador, of carrying their children in them. We were told that these women sometimes put their children there to sleep; but the custom must be rare among them, as we never saw it practised. These boots, however, form their principal pockets, and pretty capacious ones they are. Here, also, as in the jackets, considerable taste is displayed in the selection of different parts of the deer-skin, alternate strips of dark and white being placed up and down the sides and front by way of ornament. The women also wear a moccasin (*Ittee-gĕgă*) over all in the winter time.

One or two persons used to wear a sort of ruff round the neck, composed of the longest white hair of the deerskin, hanging down over the bosom in a manner very becoming to young people. It seemed to afford so little additional warmth to persons already well clothed, that I am inclined rather to attribute their wearing it to some superstitious notion. The children between two and p. 116eight or nine years of age had a pair of breeches and boots united in one, with braces over their shoulders to keep them up. These, with a jacket like the others and a pair of deer-skin mittens, with which each individual is furnished, constitute the whole of their dress. Children's clothes are often made of the skins of very young fawns and of the marmot, as being softer than those of the deer.

The Esquimaux, when thus equipped, may at all times bid defiance to the rigour of this inhospitable climate; and nothing can exceed the comfortable appearance which they exhibit even in the most inclement weather. When seen at a little distance the white rim of their hoods, whitened still more by the breath collecting and freezing upon it, and contrasted with the dark faces which they encircle, render them very grotesque objects; but while the skin of their dresses continues in good condition they always look clean and wholesome.

To judge by the eagerness with which the women received our beads, especially small white ones, as well as any other article of that kind, we might suppose them very fond of personal ornament. Yet of all that they obtained from us in this way at Winter Island, scarcely anything ever made its appearance again during our stay there, except a ring or two on the finger, and some bracelets of beads round the wrist: the latter of these was probably considered as a charm of some kind or other. We found among them, at the time of our first intercourse, a number of small black and white glass beads, disposed alternately on a string of sinew, and worn in this manner. They would also sometimes hang a small bunch of these, or a button or two, in front of their jackets and hair; and many of them, in the course of the p. 117second winter, covered the whole front of their jackets with the beads they received from us.

The most common ornament of this kind, exclusively their own, consists in strings of teeth, sometimes many hundred in number, which are either attached to the lower part of the jacket, like the fringe before described, or fastened as a belt round the waist. Most of these teeth are of the fox and wolf, but some also belong to the musk-ox (*ōŏmĭngmŭk*), of which animal, though it is never seen at Winter Island, we procured from the Esquimaux several of the grinders and a quantity of the hair and skin. The bones of the *kāblĕĕ-ārioo*, supposed to be the wolverine, constitute another of their ornaments; and it is more than probable that all these possess some imaginary qualities, as specific charms for various purposes. The most extraordinary amulet, if it be one, of this kind was a row of foxes' noses attached to the fore-part of a woman's jacket like a tier of black buttons. I purchased from Iligliuk a semicircular ornament of brass, serrated at the upper edge and brightly polished, which she wore over her hair in front and which was very becoming. The handsomest thing of this kind, however, was understood to be worn on the head by men, though we did not learn on what occasions. It consisted of a band two inches in breadth, composed of several strips of skin sewn together, alternately black and yellow; near the upper edge some hair was artfully interwoven, forming with the skin a very pretty chequer-work: along the lower edge were suspended more than a hundred small teeth, principally of the deer, neatly fastened by small double tags of sinew, and forming a very appropriate fringe.

Among their personal ornaments must also be reckoned p. 118that mode of marking the body called tattooing, which, of the customs not essential to the comfort or happiness of mankind, is perhaps the most extensively practised throughout the world. Among those people it seems to be an ornament of indispensable importance to the women, not one of them being without it. The operation is performed about the age of ten, or sometimes earlier, and has nothing to do with marriage, except that, being considered in the light of a personal charm, it may serve to recommend them as wives. The parts of the body thus marked are their faces, arms, hands, thighs, and in some few women the breasts, but never the feet as in Greenland. The operation, which by way of curiosity most of our gentlemen had practised on their arms, is very expeditiously managed by passing a needle and thread (the latter covered with lamp-black and oil) under the epidermis, according to a pattern previously marked out upon the skin. Several stitches being thus taken at once, the thumb is pressed upon the part while the thread is drawn through, by which means the colouring matter is retained, and a permanent dye of a blue tinge imparted to the skin. A woman expert at this business will perform it very quickly and with great regularity, but seldom without drawing blood in many places, and occasioning some inflammation. Where so large a portion of the surface of the body is to be covered, it must become a painful as well as tedious process, especially as, for want of needles, they often use a strip of whalebone as a substitute. For those parts where a needle cannot conveniently be passed under the skin they use the method by puncture, which is common in other countries, and by which our seamen frequently mark their hands and arms. Several of the men were marked on the back part of p. 119their hands; and with them we understood it to be considered as a souvenir of some distant or deceased person who had performed it.

In their winter habitations, I have before mentioned that the only materials employed are snow and ice, the latter being made use of for the windows alone. The work is commenced by cutting from a drift of hard and compact snow a number of oblong slabs, six or seven inches thick and about two feet in length, and laying them edgeways on a level spot, also covered with snow, in a circular form, and of a diameter from eight to fifteen feet, proportioned to the number of occupants the hut is to contain. Upon this as a foundation is laid a second tier of the same kind, but with the pieces inclining a little inwards, and made to fit closely to the lower slabs and to each other, by running a knife adroitly along the under part and sides. The top of this tier is now prepared for the reception of a third by squaring it off smoothly with a knife, all which is dexterously performed by one man standing within the circle and receiving the blocks of snow from those employed in cutting them without. When the wall has attained a height of four or five feet, it leans so much inward as to appear as if about to tumble every moment; but the workmen still fearlessly lay their blocks of snow upon it, until it is too high any longer to furnish the materials to the builder in this manner. Of this he gives notice by cutting a hole close to the ground in that part where the door is intended to be, which is near the south side, and through this the snow is now passed. Thus they continue till they have brought the sides nearly to meet in a perfect and well-constructed dome, sometimes nine or ten feet high in the centre; and this they take considerable p. 120care in finishing, by fitting the last block or keystone very nicely in the centre, dropping it into its place from the outside, though it is still done by the man within. The people outside are in the meantime occupied in throwing up snow with the *pŏoāllĕrāy*, or snow-shovel, and in stuffing in little wedges of snow where holes have been accidentally left.

The builder next proceeds to let himself out by enlarging the proposed doorway into the form of a Gothic arch three feet high, and two feet and a half wide at the bottom, communicating with which they construct two passages, each from ten to twelve feet long and from four to five feet in height, the lowest being that next the hut. The roofs of these passages are sometimes arched, but more generally made flat by slabs laid on horizontally. In first digging the snow for building the hut, they take it principally from the part where the passages are to be made, which purposely brings the floor of the latter considerably lower than that of the hut, but in no part do they dig till the bare ground appears.

The work just described completes the walls of a hut, if a single apartment only be required; but if, on account of relationship, or from any other cause, several families are to reside under one roof, the passages are made common to all, and the first apartment (in that case made smaller) forms a kind of ante-chamber, from which you go through an arched doorway, five feet high, into the inhabited apartments. When there are three of these, which is generally the case, the whole building, with its adjacent passages, forms a tolerably regular cross.

For the admission of light into the huts a round hole is cut on one side of the roof of each apartment, and a circular plate of ice, three or four inches thick and two p. 121feet in diameter, let into it. The light is soft and pleasant, like that transmitted through ground glass, and is quite sufficient for every purpose. When after some time these edifices become surrounded by drift, it is only by the windows, as I have before remarked, that they could be recognised as human habitations. It may, perhaps, then be imagined how singular is their external appearance at night, when they discover themselves only by a circular disc of light transmitted through the windows from the lamps within.

The next thing to be done is to raise a bank of snow, two and a half feet high, all round the interior of each apartment, except on the side next the door. This bank, which is neatly squared off, forms their beds and fireplace, the former occupying the sides, and the latter the end opposite the door. The passage left open up to the fireplace is between three and four feet wide. The beds are arranged by first covering the snow with a quantity of small stones, over which are laid their paddles, tent-poles, and some blades of whalebone; above these they place a number of little pieces of network, made of thin slips of whalebone, and, lastly, a quantity of twigs of birch and of the *andromeda tetragona*. Their deer-skins, which are very numerous, can now be spread without risk of their touching the snow; and such a bed is capable of affording not merely comfort but luxurious repose, in spite of the rigour of the climate. The skins thus used as blankets are made of a large size, and bordered, like some of the jackets, with a fringe of long narrow slips of leather, in which state a blanket is called *kēipik*.

The fire belonging to each family consists of a single lamp, or shallow vessel of *lapis ollaris*, its form being the lesser segment of a circle. The wick, composed of p. 122dry moss rubbed between the hands till it is quite inflammable, is disposed along the edge of the lamp on the straight side, and a greater or smaller quantity lighted, according to the heat required or the fuel that can be afforded. When the whole length of this, which is sometimes above eighteen inches, is kindled, it affords a most brilliant and beautiful light, without any perceptible smoke or any offensive smell. The lamp is made to supply itself with oil, by suspending a long thin slice of whale, seal, or sea-horse blubber near the flame, the warmth of which causes the oil to drip into the vessel until the whole is extracted. Immediately over the lamp is fixed a rude and rickety framework of wood, from which their pots are suspended, and serving also to sustain a large hoop of bone, having a net stretched tight within it. This contrivance, called *Innĕtăt*, is intended for the reception of any wet things, and is usually loaded with boots, shoes, and mittens.

The fireplace, just described as situated at the upper end of the apartment, has always two lamps facing different ways, one for each family occupying the corresponding bed-place. There is frequently also a smaller and less-pretending establishment on the same model — lamp, pot, net, and all — in one of the corners next the door; for one apartment sometimes contains three families, which are always closely related, and no married woman, or even a widow without children, is without her separate fireplace.

With all the lamps lighted and the hut full of people and dogs, a thermometer placed on the net over the fire indicated a temperature of 380; when removed two or three feet from this situation it fell to 310, and placed close to the wall stood at 230, the temperature of the open p. 123air at the time being 250 below zero. A greater degree of warmth than this produces extreme inconvenience by the dropping from the roofs. This they endeavour to obviate by applying a little piece of snow to the place from which a drop proceeds, and this adhering is for a short time an effectual remedy; but for several weeks in the spring, when the weather is too warm for these edifices, and still too cold for tents, they suffer much on this account.

The most important perhaps of the domestic utensils, next to the lamp already described, are the *ōōtkŏŏsĕĕks* or stone pots for cooking. These are hollowed out of solid *lapis ollaris*, of an oblong form, wider at the top than at the bottom, all made in similar proportion, though of various sizes, corresponding with the dimensions of the lamp which burns under it. The pot is suspended by a line of sinew at each end to the framework over the fire, and thus becomes so black on every side that the original colour of the stone is in no part discernible. Many of them were cracked quite across in several places, and mended by sewing with sinew or rivets of copper, iron, or lead, so as, with the assistance of a lashing and a due proportion of dirt, to render them quite water-tight. I may here remark that as these people distinguish the Wager River by the name of *Oōtkŏŏsĕĕksălik*, we were at first led to conjecture that they procured their pots, or the material for making them, in that neighbourhood;

this, however, they assured us was not the case, the whole of them coming from Akkoolee, where the stone is found in very high situations. One of the women at Winter Island, who came from that country, said that her parents were much employed in making these pots, chiefly it seems as articles of barter. The asbestos, which they use in the shape of a roundish pointed stick called *tatko* for p. 124trimming the lamps, is met with about Repulse Bay, and generally, as they said, on low land.

Besides the ootkooseeks, they have circular and oval vessels of whalebone of various sizes, which, as well as their ivory knives made out of a walrus's tusk, are precisely similar to those described on the western coast of Baffin's Bay in 1820. They have also a number of smaller vessels of skin sewed neatly together, and a large basket of the same material, resembling a common sieve in shape, but with the bottom close and tight, is to be seen in every apartment. Under every lamp stands a sort of "save-all," consisting of a small skin basket for catching the oil that falls over. Almost every family was in possession of a wooden tray very much resembling those used to carry butcher's meat in England, and of nearly the same dimensions, which we understood them to have procured by way of Noowook. They had a number of the bowls or cups already once or twice alluded to as being made out of the thick root of the horn of the musk-ox. Of the smaller part of the same horn they also form a convenient drinking-cup, sometimes turning it up artificially about one-third from the point, so as to be almost parallel to the other part, and cutting it full of small notches as a convenience in grasping it. These, or any other vessels for drinking, they call *Immōōchiuk*.

Besides the ivory knives, the men were well supplied with a much more serviceable kind, made of iron, and called *panna*. The form of this knife is very peculiar, being seven inches long, two and a quarter broad, quite straight and flat, pointed at the end, and ground equally sharp at both edges; this is firmly secured into a handle of bone or wood, about a foot long, by two or three iron rivets, and has all the appearance of a most destructive p. 125spearhead, but is nevertheless put to no other purpose than that of a very useful knife, which the men are scarcely ever without, especially on their sealing excursions. For these, and several knives of European form, they are probably indebted to an indirect communication with our factories in Hudson's Bay. The same may be observed of the best of their women's knives (*ooloo*), on one of which, of a larger size than usual, were the names of "Wild and Sorby." When of their own manufacture, the only iron part was a little narrow slip let into the bone and secured by rivets. It is curious to observe in this, and in numerous other instances, how exactly, amidst all the diversity of time and place, these people have preserved unaltered their manners and habits as mentioned by Crantz. That which an absurd dread of innovation does in China, the want of intercourse with other nations has effected among the Esquimaux.

Of the horn of the musk-ox they make also very good spoons much like ours in shape; and I must not omit to mention their marrow spoons (*pattēkniuk*, from *pāttĕk*, marrow), made out of long, narrow, hollowed pieces of bone, of which every housewife has a bunch of half a dozen or more tied together, and generally attached to her needle-case.

For the purpose of obtaining fire the Esquimaux use two lumps of common iron pyrites, from which sparks are struck into a little leathern case containing moss well dried and rubbed between the hands. If this tinder does not readily catch, a small quantity of the white floss of the seed of the ground willow is laid above the moss. As soon as a spark has caught, it is gently blown till the fire has spread an inch around, when, the pointed end of a piece of oiled wick being applied, it soon bursts into a p. 126flame, the whole process having occupied perhaps two or three minutes.

Among the articles in their possession, which must have been obtained by communication along shore with Hudson's Bay, were two large copper kettles, several open knives with crooked wooden handles, and many fragments of copper, iron, and old files. On a small European axe was observed the name of "Foster."

In enumerating the articles of their food, we might perhaps give a list of every animal inhabiting these regions, as they certainly will at times eat any one of them. Their principal dependence, however, is on the reindeer (*tōōktoŏ*), musk-ox (*ōōmĭngmŭk*)(in the parts where this animal is found), whale (*āggăwĕk*), walrus (*ēi-ŭ-ĕk*), the large and small seal (*ōgŭke* and *nēitiek*), and two sorts of salmon, the *ēwĕe-*

tărŏke (*salmo alpinus*?) and *ichlūŏwŏke*. The latter is taken by hooks in freshwater lakes, and the former by spearing in the shoal water of certain inlets of the sea. Of all these animals they can only procure in the winter the walrus and small seal upon this part of the coast; and these at times, as we have seen, in scarcely sufficient quantity for their subsistence.

They certainly in general prefer eating their meat cooked, and while they have fuel they usually boil it; but this is a luxury and not a necessary to them. Oily as the nature of their principal food is, yet they commonly take an equal proportion of lean to their fat, and unless very hungry do not eat it otherwise. Oil they seldom or never use in any way as a part of their general diet; and even our butter, of which they were fond, they would not eat without a due quantity of bread. They do not like salt meat as well as fresh, and never use salt themselves; but ship's pork, or even a red herring, did not come amiss p. 127to them. Of pea-soup they would eat as much as the sailors could afford to give them; and that word was the only one, with the exception of our names, which many of them ever learned in English. Among their own luxuries must be mentioned a rich soup called *kāyŏ*, made of blood, gravy, and water, and eaten quite hot. In obtaining the names of several plants, we learned that they sometimes eat the leaves of sorrel (*kōngŏlek*), and those of the ground willow; as also the red berries (*paōōna-rootik*) of the *vaccinium uliginosum*, and the root of the *potentilla pulchella*; but these cannot be said to form a part of their regular diet; scurvy grass they never eat.

Their only drink is water; and of this, when they can procure it, they swallow an inconceivable quantity; so that one of the principal occupations of the women during the winter is the thawing of snow in the ootkooseks for this purpose. They cut it into thin slices, and are careful to have it clean, on which account they will bring it from a distance of fifty yards from the huts. They have an extreme dislike to drinking water much above the temperature of 320. In eating their meals the mistress of the family, having previously cooked the meat, takes a large lump out of the pot with her fingers, and hands it to her husband, who placing a part of it between his teeth cuts it off with a large knife in that position, and then passes the knife and meat together to his next neighbour. In cutting off a mouthful of meat the knife passes so close to their lips, that nothing but constant habit could ensure them from the danger of the most terrible gashes; and it would make an English mother shudder to see the manner in which children, five or six years old, are at all times freely trusted with a knife to be used in this way.

p. 128The length of one of the best of seven canoes belonging to these Esquimaux was twenty-five feet, including a narrow-pointed projection, three feet long at each end, which turns a little upward from the horizontal. The extreme breadth, which is just before the circular hole, was twenty-one inches, and the depth ten inches and a half. The plane of the upper surface of the canoe, except in the two extreme projections, bends downwards a little from the centre towards the head and stern, giving it the appearance of what is in ships called "broken-backed." The gunwales are of fir, in some instances of one piece, three or four inches broad in the centre and tapering gradually away towards the ends. The timbers, as well as the fore-and-aft connecting pieces, are of the same material, the former being an inch square, and sometimes so close together as to require between forty and fifty of them in one canoe: which when thus "in frame" is one of the prettiest things of the kind that can be imagined. The skin with which the canoe is covered is exclusively that of the *neitiek*, prepared by scraping off the hair and fat with an *ooloo*, and stretching it tight on a frame over the fire; after which and a good deal of chewing, it is sewn on by the women with admirable neatness and strength. Their paddles have a blade at each end, the whole length being nine feet and a half; the blades are covered with a narrow plate of bone round the ends to secure them from splitting: they are always made of fir, and generally of several pieces scarfed and woolded together.

In summer they rest their canoes upon two small stones raised four feet from the ground; and in winter, on a similar structure of snow; in one case to allow them to dry freely, and in the other to prevent the snow-drift p. 129from covering, and the dogs from eating them. The difficulty of procuring a canoe may be concluded from the circumstance of there being at Winter Island twenty men able to manage one, and only seven canoes among them. Of these indeed only three or four were in good repair, the rest being wholly or in part stripped of the skin, of which a good deal was occasionally cut off during the winter, to make boots, shoes, and mittens for our people. We found no *oomiak*, or women's boat, among them, and understood that they were not in the habit of using them, which may in part be accounted for by their passing so much of the summer in the interior; they knew very well, however, what they were, and made some clumsy models of them for our people.

In the weapons used for killing their game there is considerable variety, according to the animal of which they are in pursuit. The most simple of these is the *ōōnăk*, which they use only for killing the small seal. It consists of a light staff of wood, four feet in length, having at one end the point of a narwhal's horn, from ten to eighteen inches long, firmly secured by rivets and wooldings; at the other end is a smaller and less effective point of the same kind. To prevent losing the ivory part in case of the wood breaking, a stout thong runs along the whole length of the wood, each end passing through a hole in the ivory, and the bight secured in several places to the staff. In this weapon, as far as it has yet been described, there is little art or ingenuity displayed; but a considerable degree of both in an appendage called *siātkŏ*, consisting of a piece of bone three inches long, and having a point of iron at one end, and at the other end a small hole or socket to receive the point of the oonak. Through the middle of this instrument is secured p. 130the *āllek*, or line of thong, of which every man has, when sealing, a couple of coils, each from four to six fathoms long, hanging at his back. These are made of the skin of the *oguke* as in Greenland, and are admirably adapted to the purpose, both on account of their strength, and the property which they possess of preserving their pliability even in the most intense frost.

When a seal is seen, the siatko is taken from a little leathern case, in which, when out of use, it is carefully enclosed, and attached by its socket to the point of the spear; in this situation it is retained by bringing the allek tight down and fastening it round the middle of the staff by what seamen call a "slippery hitch," which may instantly be disengaged by pulling on the other end of the line. As soon as the spear has been thrown, and the animal struck, the siatko is thus purposely separated; and being slung by the middle, now performs very effectually the important office of a barb, by turning at right angles to the direction in which it has entered the orifice. This device is in its principle superior even to our barb; for the instant any strain is put upon the line it acts like a toggle, opposing its length to a wound only as wide as its own breadth.

The *āklĕak*, or *aklēēgă*, used for the large seal, has a blown bladder attached to the staff, for the purpose of impeding the animal in the water. The weapon with two long parallel prongs of bone or iron, obtained from the natives of the Savage Islands, these people also called *akleak*, and said it was for killing seals.

The third and largest weapon is that called *katteelik*, with which the walrus and whale are attacked. The staff of this is not longer but much stouter than that of the others, especially towards the middle, where there is p. 131a small shoulder of ivory securely lashed to it for the thumb to rest against, and thus to give additional force in throwing or thrusting the spear. The ivory point of this weapon is made to fit into a socket at the end of the staff, where it is secured by double thongs, in such a manner as steadily to retain its position when a strain is put upon it in the direction of its length, but immediately disengaging itself with a sort of spring, when any lateral strain endangers its breaking. The siatko is always used with this spear; and to the end of the allek, when the animal pursued is in open water, they attach a whole seal-skin (*hŏw-wūt-tă*), inflated like a bladder, for the purpose of tiring it out in its progress through the water.

They have a spear called *īppoo* for killing deer in the water. They described it as having a light staff and a small head of iron, but they had none of these so fitted in the winter. The *nūgŭee*, or dart for birds, has, besides its two ivory prongs at the end of the staff, three divergent ones in the middle of it, with several small double barbs upon them turning inwards; they differ from the *nuguit* of Greenland, and that of the Savage Islands, in having these prongs always of unequal lengths. To give additional velocity to the bird-dart, they use a throwing-stick (*noke-shak*) which is probably the same as the "hand-board" figured by Crantz. It consists of a flat board about eighteen inches in length, having a groove to receive the staff, two others and a hole for the fingers and thumb, and a small spike fitted for a hole in the end of the staff. This instrument is used for the bird-dart only. The spear for salmon or other fish, called kākĕe-wĕi, consists of a wooden staff with a spike of bone or ivory, three inches long, secured at one end. On each p. 132side of the spike is a curved prong, much like that of a pitchfork, but made of flexible horn, which gives them a spring, and having a barb on the inner part of the point turning downwards. Their fish-hooks (*kakliōkia*) consist only of a nail crooked and pointed at one end, the other being let into a piece of ivory to which the line is attached. A piece of deer's horn or curved bone, only a foot long, is used as a rod, and completes this very rude part of their fishing-gear.

Of their mode of killing seals in the winter I have already spoken in the course of the foregoing narrative, as far as we were enabled to make ourselves acquainted with it. In their summer exploits on the water, the killing of the whale is the most arduous undertaking which they have to perform; and one cannot sufficiently admire the courage and activity which, with gear apparently so inadequate, it must require to accomplish this business. Okotook, who was at the killing of two whales in the course of a single summer, and who described the whole of it quite *con amore*, mentioned the names of thirteen men who, each in his canoe, had assisted on one of these occasions. When a fish is seen lying on the water, they cautiously paddle up astern of him, till a single canoe, preceding the rest, comes close to him on one quarter, so as to enable the man to drive the *katteelik* into the animal with all the force of both arms. This having the *siatko*, a long *allek*, and the inflated seal-skin attached to it, the whale immediately dives, taking the whole apparatus with him except the *katteelik* which, being disengaged in the manner before described, floats to the surface and is picked up by its owner. The animal re-appearing after some time, all the canoes again paddle towards him, some warning being p. 133given by the seal-skin buoy floating on the surface. Each man being furnished like the first, they repeat the blows as often as they find opportunity, till perhaps every line has been thus employed. After pursuing him in this manner, sometimes for half a day, he is at length so wearied by the resistance of the buoys, and exhausted by loss of blood, as to be obliged to rise more and more often to the surface, when, by frequent wounds with their spears, they succeed in killing him, and tow their prize in triumph to the shore. It is probable that with the whale, as with the smaller sea-animals, some privilege or perquisite is given to the first striker; and, like our own fishermen, they take a pride in having it known that their spear has been the first to inflict a wound. They meet with the most whales on the coast of *Einwĩllik*.

In attacking the walrus in the water they use the same gear, but with much more caution than with the whale, always throwing the *katteelik* from some distance, lest the animal should attack the canoe and demolish it with his tusks. The walrus is in fact the only animal with which they use any caution of this kind. They like the flesh better than that of the seal; but venison is preferred by them to either of these, and indeed to any other kind of meat.

At Winter Island they carefully preserved the heads of all the animals killed during the winter, except two or three of the walrus, which we obtained with great difficulty. There is probably some superstition attached to this, but they told us that they were to be thrown into the sea in the summer, which a Greenlander studiously avoids doing; and, indeed, at Igloolik, they had no objection to part with them before the summer arrived. As the blood of the animals which they kill is all used as p. 134food of the most luxurious kind, they are careful to avoid losing any portion of it; for this purpose they carry with them on their excursions a little instrument of ivory called *tŏopōōtă*, in form and size exactly resembling a "twenty-penny" nail, with which they stop up the orifice made by the spear, by thrusting it through the skin by the sides of the wound, and securing it with a twist. I must here also mention a simple little instrument called *keipkūttuk*, being a slender rod of bone nicely rounded, and having a point at one end and a knob or else a laniard at the other. The use of this is to thrust through the ice where they have reason to believe a seal is at work underneath. This little instrument is sometimes made as delicate as a fine wire, that the seal may not see it; and a part still remaining above the surface informs the fishermen by its motion whether the animal is employed in making his hole: if not, it remains undisturbed, and the attempt is given up in that place.

One of the best of their bows was made of a single piece of fir, four feet eight inches in length, flat on the inner side and rounded on the outer, being five inches in girth about the middle, where, however, it is strengthened on the concave side, when strung, by a piece of bone ten inches long, firmly secured by tree-nails of the same material. At each end of the bow is a knob of bone, or sometimes of wood covered with leather, with a deep notch for the reception of the string. The only wood which they can procure not possessing sufficient elasticity combined with strength, they ingeniously remedy the defect by securing to the back of the bow, and to the knobs at each end, a quantity of small lines, each composed of a plait or "sinnet" of three sinews. The number of lines thus reaching from end to end is generally about p. 135thirty; but besides these, several others are fastened with hitches round the bow, in pairs, commencing eight inches from one end, and again united at the same distance from the other, making the whole number of strings, in the middle of the bow sometimes amount to sixty. These being put on with the bow somewhat bent the contrary way, produce a spring so strong as to require considerable force as well as knack in stringing it and giving the requisite velocity to the arrow. The bow is completed by a woolding round the middle and a wedge or two, here and there, driven in to tighten it. A bow in one piece is, however, very rare; they generally consist of from two to five pieces of bone of unequal lengths, secured together by rivets and tree-nails.

The arrows vary in length from twenty to thirty inches, according to the materials that can be commanded. About two-thirds of the whole length is of fir rounded, and the rest of bone let by a socket into the wood, and having a head of thin iron, or more commonly of slate, secured into a slit by two tree-nails. Towards the opposite end of the arrow are two feathers, generally of the spotted oval, not very neatly lashed on. The bow-string consists of from twelve to eighteen small lines of three-sinew sinnet, having a loose twist, and with a separate becket of the same size for going over the knobs at the end of the bow.

We tried their skill in archery by getting them to shoot at a mark for a prize, though with bows in extremely bad order, on account of the frost, and their hands very cold. The mark was two of their spears stuck upright in the snow, their breadth being three inches and a half. At twenty yards they struck this every time; at thirty, sent the arrows always within an inch or two of it; and at forty or fifty yards, I should think, would generally hit p. 136a fawn if the animal stood still. These weapons are perhaps sufficient to inflict a mortal wound at something more than that distance, for which, however, a strong arm would be required. The animals which they kill with the bow and arrow for their subsistence are principally the musk-ox and deer, and less frequently the bear, wolf, fox, hare, and some of the smaller animals.

It is a curious fact that the musk-ox is very rarely found to extend his migrations to the eastward of a line passing through Repulse Bay, or about the meridian of 860 west, while in a northern direction we know that he travels as far as the seventy-sixth degree of latitude. In Greenland this animal is known only by vague and exaggerated report; on the western coast of Baffin's Bay it has certainly been seen, though very rarely, by the present inhabitants; and the eldest person belonging to the Winter Island tribe had never seen one to the eastward of Eiwillik, where, as well as at Akkōōleĕ, they are said to be numerous on the banks of fresh-water lakes and streams. The few men who had been present at the killing of one of these creatures seemed to pride themselves very much upon it. Toolooak, who was about seventeen years of age, had never seen either the musk-ox or the *kābleĕ-ārioo*, a proof that the latter also is not common in this corner of America.

The reindeer are killed by the Esquimaux in great abundance in the summer season, partly by driving them from islands or narrow necks of land into the sea, and then spearing them from their canoes; and partly by shooting them from behind heaps of stones raised for the purpose of watching them and imitating their peculiar bellow or grunt. Among the various artifices which they employ for this purpose, one of the most ingenious p. 137consists in two men walking directly from the deer they wish to kill, when the animal almost always follows them. As soon as they arrive at a large stone, one of the men hides behind it with his bow, while the other, continuing to walk on, soon leads the deer within range of his companion's arrows. They are also very careful to keep to leeward of the deer, and will scarcely go out after them at all when the weather is calm. For several weeks in the course of the summer some of these people almost entirely give up their fishery on the coast, retiring to the banks of lakes several miles in the interior, which they represent as large and deep and abounding with salmon, while the pasture near them affords good feeding to numerous herds of deer.

The distance to which these people extend their inland migrations, and the extent of coast of which they possess a personal knowledge, are really very considerable. Of these we could at the time of our first intercourse form no correct judgment, from our uncertainty as to the length of what they call a *seenik* (sleep), or one day's journey, by which alone they could describe to us, with the help of their imperfect arithmetic, the distance from one place to another. But our subsequent knowledge of the coast has cleared up much of this difficulty, affording the means of applying to their hydrographical sketches a tolerably accurate scale for those parts which we have not hitherto visited. A great number of these people, who were born at Amitioke and Igloolik, had been to *Noowook*, or nearly as far south as Chesterfield Inlet, which is about the *ne plus ultra* of their united knowledge in a southerly direction. Not one of them had been by water round to Akkoolee, but several by land; in which mode of travelling they only consider that country p. 138from three to five days' journey from Repulse Bay. Okotook and a few others of the Winter Island tribe had extended their peregrinations a considerable distance to the northward, over the large insular piece of land to which we have applied the name of Cockburn Island; which they described as high land and the resort of numerous reindeer. Here Okotook informed us he had seen icebergs, which these people call by a name (*pīccălōōyăk*) having in its pronunciation some affinity to that used in Greenland. By the information afterwards obtained when nearer the spot, we had reason to suppose this land must reach beyond the seventy-second degree of latitude in a northerly direction; so that these people possess a personal knowledge of the continent of America and its adjacent islands, from that parallel to Chesterfield Inlet in 63>0, being a distance of more than five hundred miles reckoned in a direct line, besides the numerous turnings and windings of the coast along which they are accustomed to travel. Ewerat and some others had been a considerable distance up the Wager River; but no record had been preserved among them of Captain Middleton's visit to that inlet about the middle of the last century.

Of the continental shore to the westward of Akkoolee, the Esquimaux invariably disclaimed the slightest personal knowledge; for no land can be seen in that direction from the hills. They entertain, however, a confused idea that neither Esquimaux nor Indians could there subsist, for want of food. Of the Indians they know enough by tradition to hold them in considerable dread, on account of their cruel and ferocious manners. When, on one occasion, we related the circumstances of the inhuman massacre described by Hearne, they crowded p. 139round us in the hut, listening with mute and almost breathless attention; and the mothers drew their children closer to them, as if to guard them from the dreadful catastrophe. It is worthy of notice that they call the Indians by a name (*Eērt-kĕi-lĕe*), which appears evidently the same as that applied by the Greenlanders to the man-eaters supposed to inhabit the eastern coast of their country, and to whom terror has assigned a face like that of a dog.

The Esquimaux take some animals in traps, and by a very ingenious contrivance of this kind they caught two wolves at Winter Island. It consists of a small house built of ice, at one end of which a door, made of the same plentiful material, is fitted to slide up and down in a groove; to the upper part of this a line is attached, and, passing over the roof, is let down into the trap at the inner end, and there held by slipping an eye in the end of it over a peg of ice left for the purpose. Over the peg, however, is previously placed a loose grummet, to which the bait is fastened, and a false roof placed over all to hide the line. The moment the animal drags at the bait the grummet slips off the peg, bringing with it the line that held up the door, and this falling down closes the trap and secures him.

A trap for birds is formed by building a house of snow just large enough to contain one person, who closes himself up in it. On the top is left a small aperture, through which the man thrusts one of his hands to secure the bird the moment he alights to take away a bait of meat laid beside it. It is principally gulls that are taken thus; and the boys sometimes amuse themselves in this manner. A trap in which they catch foxes has been mentioned in another place.

p. 140The sledges belonging to these Esquimaux were in general large and heavily constructed, being more adapted to the carriage of considerable burdens than to very quick travelling. They varied in size, being from six and a half to nine feet in length, and from eighteen inches to two feet in breadth. Some of those at Igloolik were of larger dimensions, one being eleven feet in length, and weighing two hundred and sixty-eight pounds, and two or three others above two hundred pounds. The runners are sometimes made of the right and left jaw-bones of a whale; but more commonly of several pieces of wood or bone scarfed and lashed together, the interstices being filled, to make all smooth and firm, with moss stuffed in tight, and then cemented by throwing water to freeze upon it. The lower part of the runner is shod with a plate of harder bone, coated with fresh-water ice to make it run smoothly and to avoid wear and tear, both which purposes are thus completely answered. This coating is performed with a mixture of snow and fresh water about half an inch thick, rubbed over it till it is quite smooth and hard upon the surface, and this is usually done a few minutes before setting out on a journey. When the ice is only in part worn off, it is renewed by taking some water into the mouth, and spirting it over the former coating. We noticed a sledge which was extremely curious, on account of one of the runners and a part of the other being constructed without the assistance of wood, iron, or bone of any kind. For this purpose a number of seal-skins being rolled up and disposed into the requisite shape, an outer coat of the same kind was sewed tightly round them; this formed the upper half of the runner, the lower part of which consisted entirely of moss moulded while wet into the p. 141proper form, and being left to freeze, adhering firmly together and to the skins. The usual shoeing of smooth ice beneath completed the runner, which for more than six months out of twelve, in this climate, was nearly as hard as any wood; and for winter use no way inferior to those constructed of more durable materials. The cross-pieces which form the bottom of the sledge are made of bone, wood, or anything they can muster. Over these is generally laid a seal-skin as a flooring, and in the summertime a pair of deer's horns are attached to the sledge as a back, which in the winter are removed to enable them when stopping to turn the sledge up, so as to prevent the dogs running away with it. The whole is secured by lashings of thong, giving it a degree of strength combined with flexibility which perhaps no other mode of fastening could effect.

The dogs of the Esquimaux, of which these people possessed above a hundred, have been so often described that there may seem little left to add respecting their external appearance, habits, and use. Our visits to Igloolik having, however, made us acquainted with some not hitherto described, I shall here offer a further account of these invaluable animals. In the form of their bodies, their short pricked ears, thick furry coat, and bushy tail, they so nearly resemble the wolf of these regions that, when of a light or brindled colour, they may easily at a little distance be mistaken for that animal. To an eye accustomed to both, however, a difference is perceptible in the wolf's always keeping his head down and his tail between his legs in running, whereas the dogs almost always carry their tails handsomely curled over the back. A difference less distinguishable, when the animals are apart, is the superior size and more muscular make of the p. 142wild animal, especially about the breast and legs. The wolf is also, in general, full two inches taller than any Esquimaux dog we have seen; but those met with in 1818, in the latitude of 760, appear to come nearest to it in that respect. The tallest dog at Igloolik stood two feet one inch from the ground, measured at the withers; the average height was about two inches less than this.

The colour of the dogs varies from a white, through brindled, to black-and-white, or almost entirely black. Some are also of a reddish or ferruginous colour, and others have a brownish-red tinge on their legs, the rest of their bodies being of a darker colour, and these last were observed to be generally the best dogs. Their hair in the winter is from three to four inches long; but besides this, Nature furnishes them during this rigorous season with a thick under-coating of close soft wool, which they begin to cast in the spring. While thus provided, they are able to withstand the most inclement weather without suffering from the cold; and at whatever temperature the atmosphere may be, they require nothing but a shelter from the wind to make them comfortable, and even this they do not always obtain. They are also wonderfully enabled to endure the cold even on those parts of the body which are not thus protected, for we have seen a young puppy sleeping, with its bare paw laid on an ice-anchor, with the thermometer at -300, which with one of our dogs would have produced immediate and intense pain, if not subsequent mortification. They never bark, but have a long melancholy howl like that of the wolf, and this they will sometimes perform in concert for a minute or two together. They are besides always snarling and fighting among one another, by which several of them are generally lame. When much p. 143caressed and well fed, they become quite familiar and domestic; but this mode of treatment does not improve their qualities as animals of draught. Being desirous of ascertaining whether these dogs are wolves in a state of domestication, a question which we understood to have been the subject of some speculation, Mr. Skeoch, at my request, made a skeleton of each, when the number of all the vertebra was found to be the same in both, and to correspond with the well-known anatomy of the wolf.

When drawing a sledge, the dogs have a simple harness (*annoo*) of deer or seal skin, going round the neck by one bight, and another for each of the fore-legs, with a single thong leading over the back and attached to the sledge as a trace. Though they appear at first sight to be huddled together without regard to regularity, there is, in fact, considerable attention paid to their arrangement, particularly in the selection of a dog of peculiar spirit and sagacity, who is allowed, by a longer trace, to precede the rest as leader, and to whom, in turning to the right or left, the driver usually addresses himself. This choice is made without regard to age or sex, and the rest of the dogs take precedency according to their training or sagacity, the least effective being put nearest the sledge. The leader is usually from eighteen to twenty feet from the fore part of the sledge, and the hindmost dog about half that distance, so that when ten or twelve are running together, several are nearly abreast of each other. The driver sits quite low on the fore part of the sledge, with his feet overhanging the snow on one side, and having in his hand a whip, of which the handle, made either of wood, bone, or whalebone, is eighteen inches, and the lash more than as many feet in length. The part of the thong next the handle is plaited a little p. 144way down to stiffen it and give it a spring, on which much of its use depends; and that which composes the lash is chewed by the women to make it flexible in frosty weather. The men acquire from their youth considerable expertness in the use of this whip, the lash of which is left to trail along the ground by the side of the sledge, and with which they can inflict a very severe blow on any dog at pleasure. Though the dogs are kept in training entirely by fear of the whip, and indeed without it would soon have their own way, its immediate effect is always detrimental to the draught of the sledge; for not only does the individual that is struck draw back and slacken his trace, but generally turns upon his next neighbour, and this, passing on to the next, occasions a general divergency, accompanied by the usual yelping and showing of teeth. The dogs then come together again by degrees, and the draught of the sledge is accelerated; but, even at the best of times, by this rude mode of draught, the traces of one-third of the dogs form an angle of thirty or forty degrees on each side of the direction in which the sledge is advancing. Another great inconvenience attending the Esquimaux method of putting the dogs to, besides that of not employing their strength to the best advantage, is the constant entanglement of the traces by the dogs repeatedly doubling under from side to side to avoid the whip, so that, after running a few miles, the traces always require to be taken off and cleared.

In directing the sledge the whip acts no very essential part, the driver for this purpose using certain words, as the carters do with us, to make the dogs turn more to the right or left. To these a good leader attends with admirable precision, especially if his own name be p. 145repeated at the same time, looking behind over his shoulder with great earnestness, as if listening to the directions of the driver. On a beaten track, or even where a single foot or sledge mark is occasionally discernible, there is not the slightest trouble in guiding the dogs; for even in the darkest night and in the heaviest snowdrift there is little or no danger of their losing the road, the leader keeping his nose near the ground, and directing the rest with wonderful sagacity. Where, however, there is no beaten track, the best driver among them makes a terribly circuitous course, as all the Esquimaux roads plainly show; these generally occupying an extent of six miles, when with a horse and sledge the journey would scarcely have amounted to five. On rough ground, as among hummocks of ice, the sledge would be frequently overturned, or altogether stopped, if the driver did not repeatedly get off, and, by lifting or drawing it to one side, steer it clear of those accidents. At all times, indeed, except on a smooth and well-made road, he is pretty constantly employed thus with his feet, which, together with his never-ceasing vociferations and frequent use of the whip, renders the driving of one of these vehicles by no means a pleasant or easy task. When the driver wishes to stop the sledge, he calls out "Wo, woa," exactly as our carters do; but the attention paid to this command depends altogether on his ability to enforce it. If the weight is small and the journey homeward, the dogs are not to be thus delayed; the driver is therefore obliged to dig his heels into the snow to obstruct their progress; and having thus succeeded in stopping them, he stands up with one leg before the foremost cross-piece of the sledge, till, by means of laying the whip gently over each dog's head, he has p. 146made them all lie down. He then takes care not to quit his position; so that should the dogs set off he is thrown upon the sledge, instead of being left behind by them.

With heavy loads the dogs draw best with one of their own people, especially a woman, walking a little way ahead; and in this case they are sometimes enticed to mend their pace by holding a mitten to the mouth, and then making the motion of cutting it with a knife, and throwing it on the snow, when the dogs, mistaking it for meat, hasten forward to pick it up. The women also entice them from the huts in a similar manner. The rate at which they travel depends, of course, on the weight they have to draw, and the road on which their journey is performed. When the latter is level and very hard and smooth, constituting what in other parts of North America is called "good sleighing," six or seven dogs will draw from eight to ten hundredweight, at the rate of seven or eight miles an hour, for several hours together, and will easily under those circumstances perform a journey of fifty or sixty miles a day; on untrodden snow, five-and-twenty or thirty miles would be a good day's journey. The same number of well-fed dogs, with a weight of only five or six hundred pounds (that of the sledge included), are almost unmanageable, and will on a smooth road run any way they please at the rate of ten miles an hour. The work performed by a greater number of dogs is, however, by no means in proportion to this, owing to the imperfect mode already described of employing the strength of these sturdy creatures, and to the more frequent snarling and fighting occasioned by an increase of numbers.

In the summer, when the absence of snow precludes the use of sledges, the dogs are still made useful on p. 147journeys and hunting excursions, by being employed to carry burdens in a kind of saddle-bags laid across their shoulders. A stout dog thus accoutred will accompany his master, laden with a weight of about twenty to twenty-five pounds. When leading the dogs, the Esquimaux take a half hitch with the trace round their necks to prevent their pulling, and the same plan is followed when a sledge is left without a keeper. They are also in the habit of tethering them, when from home, by tying up one of the fore-legs; but a still more effectual method is similar to that which we saw employed by the Greenlanders of Prince Regent's Bay, and consists in digging with their spears two holes in the ice in an oblique direction and meeting each other, so as to leave an eye-bolt, to which the dogs are fastened.

The scent of the Esquimaux dogs is excellent; and this property is turned to account by their masters in finding the seal holes, which these invaluable animals will discover entirely by the smell at a very great distance. The track of a single deer upon the snow will in like manner set them off at a full gallop, when travelling, at least a quarter of a mile before they arrive at it, when they are with difficulty made to turn in any other direction; and the Esquimaux are accustomed to set them after those animals to hunt them down when already wounded with an arrow. In killing bears the dogs act a very essential part, and two or three of them when led on by a man will eagerly attack one of those ferocious creatures. An Esquimaux seldom uses any other weapon than his spear and *panna* in this encounter, for which the readiness of the dogs may be implied from the circumstance of the word "nennook" (bear), being often used to encourage them when running in a sledge. Indeed, the only animal p. 148which they are not eager to chase is the wolf, of which the greater part of them seem to have an instinctive dread, giving notice at night of their approach to the huts by a loud and continued howl. There is not one dog in twenty among them that will voluntarily, or indeed without a great deal of beating, take the water if they think it is out of their depth, and the few that would do so were spoken of as extraordinary exceptions.

The Esquimaux in general treat their dogs much as an unfeeling master does his slaves; that is, they take just as much care of them as their own interest is supposed to require. The bitches with young are in the winter allowed to occupy a part of their own beds, where they are carefully attended and fed by the women, who will even supply the young ones with meat and water from their mouths as they do their own children, and not unfrequently also carry them in their hoods to take care of them. It is probably on this account that the dogs are always so much attached to the women, who can at any time catch them or entice them from the huts when the men fail. Two females that were with young on board the *Fury* in the month of February brought forth six and seven at a litter, and the former number were all females. Their feeding, which, both in summer and winter, principally consists of *kāŏw*, or the skin and part of the blubber of the walrus, is during the latter season very precarious, their masters having then but little to spare. They therefore become extremely thin at that time of the year, and would scarcely be recognised as the same animals as when regularly fed in the summer. No wonder therefore that they will eat almost anything however tough or filthy, and that neither whipping nor shouting will prevent their turning out of the road, even p. 149when going at full speed, to pick up whatever they espy. When at the huts they are constantly creeping in to pilfer what they can, and half the time of the people sitting there is occupied in vociferating their names and driving them by most unmerciful blows out of the apartments. The dogs have no water to drink during the winter, but lick up some clean snow occasionally as a substitute; nor indeed if water be offered them do they care about it unless it happens to be oily. They take great pleasure in rolling in clean snow, especially after or during a journey, or when they have been confined in a house during the night. Notwithstanding the rough treatment which they receive from their masters their attachment to them is very great, and this they display after a short absence by jumping up and licking their faces all over with extreme delight. The Esquimaux, however, never caress them, and indeed scarcely ever take any notice of them but when they offend, and they are not then sparing in their blows. The dogs have all names, to which they attend with readiness, whether drawing in a sledge or otherwise. Their names are frequently the same as those of the people, and in some instances are given after the relations of their masters, which seems to be considered an act of kindness among them. Upon the whole, notwithstanding the services performed by these valuable creatures, I am of opinion that art cannot well have done less towards making them useful, and that the same means in almost any other hands would be employed to greater advantage.

*****

In the disposition of these people, there was of course among so many individuals considerable variety as to p. 150the minute points; but in the general features of their character, which with them are not subject to the changes produced by foreign intercourse, one description will nearly apply to all. The virtue which, as respected ourselves, we could most have wished them to possess is honesty, and the impression derived from the early part of our intercourse was certainly in this respect a favourable one. A great many instances occurred, some of which have been related, where they appeared even scrupulous in returning articles that did not belong to them; and this too when detection of a theft, or at least of the offender, would have been next to impossible. As they grew more familiar with us, and the temptations became stronger, they gradually relaxed in their honesty, and petty thefts were from time to time committed by several individuals both male and female among them.

The bustle which any search for stolen goods occasioned at the huts was a sufficient proof of their understanding the estimation in which the crime was held by us. Until the affair was cleared up they would affect great readiness to show every article which they had got from the ships, repeating the name of the donor with great warmth, as if offended at our suspicions, yet with a half-smile on their countenances at our supposed credulity in believing them. There was, indeed, at all times some degree of trick and cunning in this show of openness and candour; and they would at times bring back some very trifling article that had been given them, tendering it as a sort of expiation for the theft of another much more valuable. When a search was making they would invent all sorts of lies to screen themselves, not caring on whom besides the imputation fell; and more than once they directed our people to the apartments of others who were innocent of the p. 151offence in question. If they really knew the offender, they were generally ready enough to inform against him, and this with an air of affected secrecy and mysterious importance; and, as if the dishonesty of another constituted a virtue in themselves, they would repeat this information frequently, perhaps for a month afterwards, setting up their neighbour's offence as a foil to their own pretended honesty.

In appreciating the character of these people for honesty, however, we must not fail to make due allowance for the degree of temptation to which they were daily exposed amidst the boundless stores of wealth which our ships appeared to them to furnish. To draw a parallel case, we must suppose a European of the lower class suffered to roam about amidst hoards of gold and silver; for nothing less valuable can be justly compared with the wood and iron that everywhere presented themselves to their view on board the ships. The European and the Esquimaux who, in cases so similar, both resist the temptation of stealing, must be considered pretty nearly on a par in the scale of honesty; and judging in this manner, the balance might possibly be found in favour of the latter when compared with any similar number of Europeans taken at random from the lower class.

In what has been hitherto said, regard has been had only to their dealings with us. In their transactions among themselves there is no doubt that, except in one or two privileged cases, such as that of destitute widows, the strictest honesty prevails, and that as regards the good of their own community they are generally honest people. We have in numberless instances sent presents by one to another, and invariably found that they had p. 152been faithfully delivered. The manner in which their various implements are frequently left outside their huts is a proof, indeed, that robbery is scarcely known among them. It is true that there is not an article in the possession of one of them of which any of the rest will not readily name the owner, and the detection of a theft would therefore be certain and immediate. Certainty of detection, however, among a lawless and ferocious people, instead of preventing robbery, would more probably add violence and murder to the first crime, and the strongest would ultimately gain the upper hand. We cannot, therefore, but admire the undisturbed security in which these people hold their property without having recourse to any restraint beyond that which is incurred by the tacitly received law of mutual forbearance.

In the barter of their various commodities their dealings with us were fair and upright, though latterly they were by no means backward or inexpert in driving a bargain. The absurd and childish exchanges which they at first made with our people induced them subsequently to complain that the Kabloonas had stolen their things, though the profit had been eventually a hundredfold in their favour. Many such complaints were made when the only fault in the purchaser had been excessive liberality, and frequently also as a retort by way of warding off the imputation of some dishonesty of their own. A trick not uncommon with the women was to endeavour to excite the commiseration and to tax the bounty of one person by relating some cruel theft of this kind that had, as they said, been practised upon them by another. One day, after I had bought a knife of Togolat, she told Captain Lyon, in a most piteous tone, that *Parree* had stolen her last *ooloo*, that she did not know what to do p. 153without one, and, at length coming to the point, begged him to give her one. Presently after this, her husband coming in and asking for something to eat, she handed him some meat accompanied by a very fine ooloo. Her son, being thus reminded of eating, made the same request, upon which a second knife was produced, and immediately after, a third of the same kind for herself. Captain Lyon, having amused himself in watching these proceedings, which so well confirmed the truth of the proverb that certain people ought to have good memories, now took the knives, one by one, out of their hands, and holding them up to Togolat, asked her if Parree had not stolen her last ooloo. A hearty laugh all round was the only notice taken by them of this direct detection of the deceit.

The confidence which they really placed in us was daily and hourly evinced by their leaving their fishing gear stuck in the snow all round the ships; and not a single instance occurred, to my knowledge, of any theft committed on their property. The licking of the articles received from us was not so common with them as with Esquimaux in general, and this practice was latterly almost entirely left off by them.

Among the unfavourable traits in their character must be reckoned an extreme disposition to envy, which displayed itself on various occasions during our intercourse with them. If we had made any presents in one hut, the inmates of the next would not fail to tell us of it, accompanying their remarks with some satirical observation, too unequivocally expressed to be mistaken, and generally by some stroke of irony directed against the favoured person. If any individual with whom we had been intimate happened to be implicated in a theft, the circumstance p. 154became a subject of satisfaction too manifest to be repressed, and we were told of it with expressions of the most triumphant exultation on every occasion. It was indeed curious, though ridiculous, to observe that, even among these simple people, and in this obscure corner of the globe, that little gossip and scandal so commonly practised in small societies among us were very frequently displayed. This was especially the case with the women, of whom it was not uncommon to see a group sitting in a hut for hours together, each relating her quota of information, now and then mimicking the persons of whom they spoke, and interlarding their stories with jokes evidently at the expense of their absent neighbours, though to their own infinite amusement.

In extenuation, however, of these faults, it must be allowed that we were ourselves the exciting cause which called them into action, and without which they would be comparatively of rare occurrence among them. Like every other child of Adam, they undoubtedly possess their share of the seeds of these human frailties; but even in this respect they need not shrink from a comparison with ourselves, for who among us can venture to assure himself that if exposed to similar temptations he would not be found wanting?

To another failing to which they are addicted the same excuse will not so forcibly apply, as in this respect our acquaintance with them naturally furnishes an opportunity for the practice of a virtue, rather than for the development of its opposite vice. I have already, in the course of the foregoing narrative, hinted at the want of gratitude evinced by these people in their transactions with us. Among themselves, almost the only case in which this sentiment can have any field for exertion is p. 155in the conduct of children towards their parents, and in this respect, as I shall presently have occasion to notice, their gratitude is by no means conspicuous. Anything like a free gift is very little, if at all, known among them. If A gives B a part of his seal to-day, the latter soon returns an equal quantity when he is the successful fisherman. Uncertain as their mode of living is, and dependent as they are upon each other's exertions, this custom is the evident and unquestionable interest of all. The regulation does credit to their wisdom, but has nothing to do with their generosity. This being the case, it might be supposed that our numerous presents, for which no return was asked, would have excited in them something like thankfulness, combined with admiration; but this was so little the case that the *coyenna* (thanks) which did now and then escape them, expressed much less than even the most common-place "thank ye" of civilised society. Some exceptions, for they were only exceptions, and rare ones, to this rule have been mentioned as they occurred; but, in general, however considerable the benefit conferred, it was forgotten in a day; and this forgetfulness was not unfrequently aggravated by their giving out that their benefactor had been so shabby as to make them no present at all. Even those individuals who, either from good behaviour or superior intelligence, had been most noticed by us, and particularly such as had slept on board the ships, and whether in health or sickness had received the most friendly treatment from everybody, were in general just as indifferent as the rest; and I do not believe that any one amongst them would have gone half a mile out of his road, or have sacrificed the most trivial self-gratification, to have served us. Though the riches lay on our side, they possessed abundant means of making some p. 156nominal return, which, for the sake of the principle that prompted it, would of course have been gratifying to us. Okotook and Iligliuk, whom I had most loaded with presents, and who had never offered me a single free gift in return, put into my hand, at the time of their first removal from Winter Island, a dirty crooked model of a spear, so shabbily constructed that it had probably been already refused as an article of barter by many of the ship's company. On my accepting this, from an unwillingness to affront them, they were uneasy and dissatisfied till I had given them something in return, though their hands were full of the presents which I had just made them. Selfishness is, in fact, almost without exception their universal characteristic, and the main-spring of all their actions, and that, too, of a kind the most direct and unamiable that can well be imagined.

In the few opportunities we had of putting their hospitality to the test, we had every reason to be pleased with them. Both as to food and accommodation, the best they had were always at our service; and their attention, both in kind and degree, was everything that hospitality and even good breeding could dictate. The kindly offices of drying and mending our clothes, cooking our provision, and thawing snow for our drink were performed by the women with an obliging cheerfulness which we shall not easily forget, and which commanded its due share of our admiration and esteem. While thus their guest, I have passed an evening not only with comfort, but with extreme gratification; for with the women working and singing, their husbands quietly mending their lines, the children playing before the door, and the pot boiling over the blaze of a cheerful lamp, one might well forget for the time that an Esquimaux hut was the scene of this p. 157domestic comfort and tranquillity; and I can safely affirm with Cartwright, that, while thus lodged beneath their roof, I know no people whom I would more confidently trust, as respects either my person or my property, than the Esquimaux. It is painful, and may perhaps be considered invidious after this, to inquire how far their hospitality would in all probability be extended if interest were wholly separated from its practice, and a stranger were destitute and unlikely soon to repay them. But truth obliges me to confess that, from the extreme selfishness of their general conduct, as well as from their behaviour in some instances to the destitute of their own tribe, I should be sorry to lie under the necessity of thus drawing very largely on their bounty.

The estimation in which women are held among these people is, I think, somewhat greater than is usual in savage life. In their general employments they are by no means the drudges that the wives of the Greenlanders are said to be; being occupied only in those cares which may properly be called domestic, and as such are considered the peculiar business of the women among the lower classes in civilised society. The wife of one of these people, for instance, makes and attends the fire, cooks the victuals, looks after the children, and is sempstress to her whole family; while her husband is labouring abroad for their subsistence. In this respect it is not even necessary to except their task of cutting up the small seals, which is, in truth, one of the greatest luxuries and privileges they enjoy; and even if it were esteemed a labour, it could scarcely be considered equivalent to that of the women in many of our own fishing-towns, where the men's business is at an end the moment the boat touches the beach. The most laborious of their tasks occurs p. 158perhaps in making their various journeys, when all their goods and chattels are to be removed at once, and when each individual must undoubtedly perform a full share of the general labour. The women are, however, good walkers, and not easily fatigued; for we have several times known a young woman of two-and-twenty, with a child in her hood, walk twelve miles to the ships and back again the same day for the sake of a little bread-dust and a tin canister. When stationary in the winter, they have really almost a sinecure of it, sitting quietly in their huts, and having little or no employment for the greater part of the day. In short, there are few, if any, people in this state of society among whom the women are so well off. They always sit upon the beds with their legs doubled under them, and are uneasy in the posture usual with us. The men sometimes sit as we do, but more generally with their legs crossed before them.

The women do not appear to be in general very prolific. Illumea, indeed, had borne seven children, but no second instance of an equal number in one family afterwards came to our knowledge; three or four is about the usual number. They are, according to their own account, in the habit of suckling their children to the age of three years; but we have seen a child of five occasionally at the breast, though they are dismissed from the mother's hood at about the former age. The time of weaning them must of course, in some instances, depend on the mother's again becoming pregnant, and if this succeeds quickly it must, as Crantz relates of the Greenlanders, go hard with one of the infants. Nature, however, seems to be kind to them in this respect, for we did not witness one instance, nor hear of any, in which a woman was put to this inconvenience and distress. It is not uncommon to see one p. 159woman suckling the child of another, while the latter happens to be employed in her other domestic occupations. They are in the habit also of feeding their younger children from their own mouths, softening the food by mastication, and then turning their heads round, so that the infant in the hood may put its lips to theirs. The chill is taken from water for them in the same manner, and some fathers are very fond of taking their children on their knees and thus feeding them. The women are more desirous of having sons than daughters, as on the former must principally depend their support in old age.

Twelve of the men had each two wives, and some of the younger ones had also two betrothed; two instances occurred of the father and son being married to sisters. The custom of betrothing children in their infancy is commonly practised here, in which respect these people differ from the natives of Greenland, where it is comparatively rare. A daughter of Arnaneelia, between two and three years old, had long been thus contracted to Okotook's son, a hero of six or seven, and the latter used to run about the hut, calling his intended by the familiar appellation of *Nŏŏllē-ă* (wife), to the great amusement of the parents. When a man has two wives, there is generally a difference of five or six years in their ages. The senior takes her station next the principal fire, which comes entirely under her management; and she is certainly considered in some respects superior to the other, though they usually live together in the utmost harmony. The men sometimes repudiate their wives without ceremony, in case of real or supposed bad behaviour, as in Greenland, but this does not often occur. There was a considerable disparity of age between many of the men and their wives, the husband being sometimes the oldest p. 160by twenty years or more, and this also when he had never married any former wife. We knew no instance in which the number of a man's wives exceeded two, and indeed we had every reason to believe that the practice is never admitted among them. We met with a singular instance of two men having exchanged wives, in consequence merely of one of the latter being pregnant at the time when her husband was about to undertake a long journey.

The authority of the husband seems to be sufficiently absolute, depending nevertheless in great measure on the dispositions of the respective parties. Iligliuk was one of those women who seemed formed to manage their husbands; and we one day saw her take Okotook to task in a very masterly style for having bartered away a good jacket for an old useless pistol without powder or shot. He attempted at first to bluster in his turn, and with most women would probably have gained his point. But with Iligliuk this would not do; she saw at once the absurdity of his bargain, and insisted on his immediately cancelling it, which was accordingly done, and no more said about it. In general, indeed, the husband maintains his authority, and in several instances of supposed bad behaviour in a wife, we saw obedience enforced in a pretty summary manner. It is very rare, however, to see them proceed to this extremity; and the utmost extent of a husband's want of tenderness towards his wife consists in general in making her walk or lead the dogs, while he takes his own seat in the sledge and rides in comfort. Widows, as might be expected, are not so well off as those whose husbands are living, and this difference is especially apparent in their clothes, which are usually very dirty, thin, and ragged; when indeed they happen to have p. 161no near relatives, their fate, as we have already seen, is still worse than this.

I fear we cannot give a very favourable account of the chastity of the women, nor of the delicacy of their husbands in this respect. As for the latter, it was not uncommon for them to offer their wives as freely for sale as a knife or a jacket. Some of the young men informed us that, when two of them were absent together on a sealing excursion, they often exchanged wives for the time, as a matter of friendly convenience; and indeed, without mentioning any other instances of this nature, it may safely be affirmed that in no country is prostitution carried to greater lengths than among these people. The behaviour of most of the women when their husbands were absent from the huts plainly evinced their indifference towards them, and their utter disregard of connubial fidelity. The departure of the men was usually the signal for throwing aside restraint, which was invariably resumed on their return. For this event they take care to be prepared by the report of the children, one of whom is usually posted on the outside for the purpose of giving due notice.

The affection of parents for their children was frequently displayed by these people, not only in the mere passive indulgence, and abstinence from corporal punishment, for which Esquimaux have before been remarked, but by a thousand playful endearments also, such as parents and nurses practise in our own country. Nothing indeed can well exceed the kindness with which they treat their children; and this trait in their character deserves to be the more insisted on, because it is in reality the only very amiable one which they possess. It must be confessed, indeed, that the gentleness and docility of p. 162the children are such as to occasion their parents little trouble, and to render severity towards them quite unnecessary. Even from their earliest infancy, they possess that quiet disposition, gentleness of demeanour, and uncommon evenness of temper, for which in more mature age they are for the most part distinguished. Disobedience is scarcely ever known, a word or even a look from a parent is enough; and I never saw a single instance of that frowardness and disposition to mischief which with our youth so often requires the whole attention of a parent to watch over and to correct. They never cry from trifling accidents, and sometimes not even from very severe hurts, at which an English child would sob for an hour. It is indeed astonishing to see the indifference with which, even as tender infants, they bear the numerous blows they accidentally receive when carried at their mothers' backs.

They are just as fond of play as any other young people, and of the same kind; only that while an English child draws a cart of wood, an Esquimaux of the same age has a sledge of whalebone; and for the superb baby-house of the former, the latter builds a miniature hut of snow, and begs a lighted wick from her mother's lamp to illuminate the little dwelling. Their parents make for them, as dolls, little figures of men and women, habited in the true Esquimaux costume, as well as a variety of other toys, many of them having some reference to their future occupations in life, such as canoes, spears, and bows and arrows. The drum or tambourine, mentioned by Crantz, is common among them, and used not only by the children, but by the grown-up people at some of their games. They sometimes serrate the edges of two strips of whalebone and whirl them round their heads, just as p. 163boys do in England to make the same peculiar humming sound. They will dispose one piece of wood on another, as an axis, in such a manner that the wind turns it round like the arms of a windmill; and so of many other toys of the same simple kind. These are the distinct property of the children, who will sometimes sell them while their parents look on, without interfering or expecting to be consulted.

When not more than eight years old the boys are taken by their fathers on their sealing excursions, where they begin to learn their future business; and even at that early age they are occasionally intrusted to bring home a sledge and dogs from a distance of several miles over the ice. At the age of eleven we see a boy with his watertight boots and moccasins, a spear in his hand, and a small coil of line at his back, accompanying the men to the fishery, under every circumstance; and from this time his services daily increase in value to the whole tribe. On our first intercourse with them we supposed that they would not unwillingly have parted with their children in consideration of some valuable present, but in this we afterwards found that we were much mistaken. Happening one day to call myself Toolooak's *attata* (father), and pretend that he was to remain with me on board the ship, I received from the old man, his father, no other answer than what seemed to be very strongly and even satirically implied, by his taking one of our gentlemen by the arm and calling him his son; thus intimating that the adoption which he proposed was as feasible and as natural as my own.

The custom of adoption is carried to very great lengths among these people, and served to explain to us several apparent inconsistencies with respect to their relationships. p. 164The adoption of a child in civilised countries has usually for its motive either a tenderness for the object itself, or some affection or pity for its deceased, helpless, or unknown parents. Among the Esquimaux, however, with whom the two first of these causes would prove but little excitement, and the last can have no place, the custom owes its origin entirely to the obvious advantage of thus providing for a man's own subsistence in advanced life; and it is consequently confined almost without exception to the adoption of sons, who can alone contribute materially to the support of an aged and infirm parent. When a man adopts the son of another as his own, he is said to "*tego*," or take him; and at whatever age this is done (though it generally happens in infancy), the child then lives with his new parents, calls them father and mother, is sometimes even ignorant of any such transfer having been made, especially if his real parents should be dead; and whether he knows it or not, is not always willing to acknowledge any but those with whom he lives. Without imputing much to the natural affection of these people for their offspring, which, like their other passions, is certainly not remarkable for its strength, there would seem, on the score of disinterestedness, a degree of consideration in a man's thus giving his son to another, which is scarcely compatible with the general selfishness of the Esquimaux character; but there is reason to suppose that the expediency of this measure is sometimes suggested by a deficiency of the mother's milk, and not unfrequently perhaps by the premature death of the real parent. The agreement seems to be always made between the fathers, and to differ in no respect from the transfer of other property, except that none can equal in value the property p. 165thus disposed of. The good sense, good fortune, or extensive claims of some individuals were particularly apparent in this way, from the number of sons they had adopted. Toolemak, deriving perhaps some advantage from his qualifications as Angetkook, had taken care to negotiate for the adoption of some of the finest male children of the tribe; a provision which now appeared the more necessary from his having lost four children of his own, besides Noogloo, who was one of his *tego'd* sons. In one of the two instances that came to our knowledge of the adoption of a female child, both its own parents were still living, nor could we ascertain the motive for this deviation from the more general custom.

In their behaviour to old people, whose age or infirmities render them useless and therefore burdensome to the community, the Esquimaux betray a degree of insensibility, bordering on inhumanity, and ill-repaying the kindness of an indulgent parent. The old man Hikkeiera, who was very ill during the winter, used to lie day after day little regarded by his wife, son, daughter, and other relatives, except that his wretched state constituted, as they well knew, a forcible claim upon our charity; and, with this view, it was sure to excite a whine of sympathy and commiseration whenever we visited or spoke of him. When, however, a journey of ten miles was to be performed over the ice, they left him to find his way with a stick in the best manner he could, while the young and robust ones were many of them drawn on sledges. There is, indeed, no doubt that, had their necessities or mode of life required a longer journey than he could thus have accomplished, they would have pushed on like the Indians and left a fellow-creature to perish. It was certainly considered incumbent on his son to support him, p. 166and he was fortunate in that son's being a very good man; but a few more such journeys to a man of seventy would not impose this incumbrance upon him much longer. Illumea, the mother of several grown-up children, lived also in the same apartment with her youngest son, and in the same hut with her other relations. She did not, however, interfere, as in Greenland, with the management of her son's domestic concerns, though his wife was half an idiot. She was always badly clothed, and even in the midst of plenty not particularly well fed, receiving everything more as an act of charity than otherwise; and she will probably be less and less attended to in proportion as she stands more in need of assistance.

122

The different families appear always to live on good terms with each other, though each preserves its own habitation and property as distinct and independent as any housekeeper in England. The persons living under one roof, who are generally closely related, maintain a degree of harmony among themselves which is scarcely ever disturbed. The more turbulent passions, which when unrestrained by religious principle or unchecked by the dread of human punishment, usually create so much havoc in the world, seem to be very seldom excited in the breasts of these people, which renders personal violence or immoderate anger extremely rare among them; and one may sit in a hut for a whole day, and never witness an angry word or look, except in driving out the dogs. If they take an offence, it is more common for them to show it by the more quiet method of sulkiness; and this they now and then tried as a matter of experiment with us. Okotook, who was often in this humour, once displayed it to some of our gentlemen in his own hut, by turning his back and frequently p. 167repeating the expression "Good-bye," as a broad hint to them to go away. Toolooak was also a little given to this mood, but never retained it long, and there was no malice mixed with his displeasure. One evening that he slept on board the *Fury* he either offended Mr. Skeoch, or thought that he had done so, by this kind of humour; at all events, they parted for the night without any formal reconciliation. The next morning Mr. Skeoch was awakened at an unusually early hour by Toolooak's entering his cabin and taking hold of his hand to shake it by way of making up the supposed quarrel. On a disposition thus naturally charitable, what might not Christian education and Christian principles effect! Where a joke is evidently intended, I never knew people more ready to join in it than these are. If ridiculed for any particularity of manner, figure, or countenance, they are sure not to be long behindhand in returning it, and that very often with interest. If we were the aggressors in this way, some ironical observation respecting the *Kabloonas* was frequently the consequence; and no small portion of wit as well as irony was at times mixed with their raillery.

In point of intellect, as well as disposition, great variety was of course perceptible among the different individuals of this tribe; but few of them were wanting in that respect. Some, indeed, possessed a degree of natural quickness and intelligence which perhaps could hardly be surpassed in the natives of any country. Iligliuk, though one of the least amiable, was particularly thus gifted. When she really wished to develop our meaning, she would desire her husband and all the rest to hold their tongues, and would generally make it out while they were puzzling their heads to no purpose. In p. 168returning her answers, the very expression of her countenance, though one of the plainest among them, was almost of itself sufficient to convey her meaning; and there was in these cases a peculiar decisive energy in her manner of speaking, which was extremely interesting. This woman would indeed have easily learned anything to which she chose to direct her attention; and had her lot been cast in a civilised country instead of this dreary region, which serves alike to "freeze the genial current of the soul" and body, she would probably have been a very clever person. For want of a sufficient object, however, neither she nor any of her companions ever learned a dozen words of English, except our names, with which it was their interest to be familiar, and which, long before we left them, any child could repeat, though in their own style of pronunciation.

Besides the natural authority of parents and husbands, these people appear to admit no kind of superiority among one another, except a certain degree of superstitious reverence for their *angetkooks*, and their tacitly following the counsel or steps of the most active seal-catcher on their hunting excursions. The word *nallegak*, used in Greenland to express "master," and "lord" in the Esquimaux translations of the Scriptures, they were not acquainted with. One of the young men at Winter Island appeared to be considered somewhat in the light of a servant to Okotook, living with the latter, and quietly allowing him to take possession of all the most valuable presents which he received from us. Being a sociable people, they unite in considerable numbers to form a settlement for the winter; but on the return of spring they again separate into several parties, each appearing to choose his own route, without regard to that p. 169of the rest, but all making their arrangements without the slightest disagreement or difference of opinion that we could ever discover. In all their movements they seem to be actuated by one simultaneous feeling that is truly admirable.

Superior as our arts, contrivances, and materials must unquestionably have appeared to them, and eager as they were to profit by this superiority, yet, contradictory as it may seem, they certainly looked upon us in many respects with profound contempt, maintaining that idea of self-sufficiency which has induced them, in common with the rest of their nation, to call themselves, by way of distinction, *Innŭee*, or mankind. One day, for instance, in securing some of the gear of a sledge, Okotook broke a part of it composed of a piece of our white line, and I shall never forget the contemptuous sneer with which he muttered in soliloquy the word "Kabloona!" in token of the inferiority of our materials to his own. It is happy, perhaps, when people possessing so few of the good things of this life can be thus contented with the little allotted them.

The men, though low in stature, are not wanting in muscular strength in proportion to their size, or in activity and hardiness. They are good and even quick walkers, and occasionally bear much bodily fatigue, wet, and cold, without appearing to suffer by it, much less to complain of it. Whatever labour they have gone through, and with whatever success in procuring game, no individual ever seems to arrogate to himself the credit of having done more than his neighbour for the general good. Nor do I conceive there is reason to doubt their personal courage, though they are too good-natured often to excite others to put that quality to the test. It p. 170is true, they will recoil with horror at the tale of an Indian massacre, and probably cannot conceive what should induce one set of men deliberately and without provocation to murder another. War is not their trade; ferocity forms no part of the disposition of the Esquimaux. Whatever manly qualities they possess are exercised in a different way, and put to a far more worthy purpose. They are fishermen, and not warriors; but I cannot call that man a coward who, at the age of one-and-twenty, will attack a Polar bear single-handed, or fearlessly commit himself to floating masses of ice which the next puff of wind may drift for ever from the shore.

If, in short, they are deficient in some of the higher virtues, as they are called, of savage life, they are certainly free also from some of its blackest vices; and their want of brilliant qualities is fully compensated by those which, while they dazzle less, do more service to society and more honour to human nature. If, for instance, they have not the magnanimity which would enable them to endure without a murmur the most excruciating torture, neither have they the ferocious cruelty that incites a man to inflict that torture on a helpless fellow-creature. If their gratitude for favours be not lively nor lasting, neither is their resentment of injuries implacable, nor their hatred deadly. I do not say there are not exceptions to this rule, though we have never witnessed any; but it is assuredly not their general character.

When viewed more nearly in their domestic relations, the comparison will, I believe, be still more in their favour. It is here as a social being, as a husband and the father of a family, promoting within his own little sphere the benefit of that community in which p. 171Providence has cast his lot, that the moral character of a savage is truly to be sought; and who can turn without horror from the Esquimaux, peaceably seated after a day of honest labour with his wife and children in their snow-built hut, to the self-willed and vindictive Indian, wantonly plunging his dagger into the bosom of the helpless woman whom nature bids him cherish and protect!

Of the few arts possessed by this simple people some account has already been given in the description of their various implements. As mechanics, they have little to boast when compared with other savages lying under equal disadvantages as to scantiness of tools and materials. As carpenters, they can scarf two pieces of wood together, secure them with pins of whalebone or ivory, fashion the timbers of a canoe, shoe a paddle, and rivet a scrap of iron into a spear or arrow head. Their principal tool is the knife (*panna*), and, considering the excellence of a great number which they possessed previous to our intercourse with them, the work they do is remarkably coarse and clumsy. Their very manner of holding and handling a knife is the most awkward that can be imagined. For the purpose of boring holes they have a drill and bow so exactly like our own that they need no further description, except that the end of the drill-handle, which our artists place against their breast, is rested by these people against a piece of wood or bone held in their mouths, and having a cavity fitted to receive it. With the use of the saw they were well acquainted, but had nothing of this kind in their possession better than a notched piece of iron. One or two small European axes were lashed to handles in a contrary direction to ours; that is, to be used like an adze, a form which, according to the observation p. 172of a traveller well qualified to judge, savages in general prefer. It was said that these people steamed or boiled wood in order to bend it for fashioning the timbers of their canoes. As fishermen or seamen, they can put on a woolding or seizing with sufficient strength and security, and are acquainted with some of the most simple and serviceable knots in use among us. In all the arts, however, practised by the men, it is observable that the ingenuity lies in the principle, not in the execution. The experience of ages has led them to adopt the most efficacious methods, but their practice as handicrafts has gone no further than absolute necessity requires; they bestow little labour upon neatness or ornament.

In some of the few arts practised by the women there is much more dexterity displayed, particularly in that important branch of a housewife's business, sewing, which even with their own clumsy needles of bone they perform with extraordinary neatness. They had, however, several steel needles of a three-cornered shape, which they kept in a very convenient case, consisting of a strip of leather passed through a hollow bone and having its ends remaining out, so that the needles which are stuck into it may be drawn in and out at pleasure. These cases were sometimes ornamented by cutting; and several thimbles of leather, one of which in sewing is worn on the first finger, are usually attached to it, together with a bunch of narrow spoons and other small articles liable to be lost. The thread they use is the sinew of the reindeer (*tooktoo ĕwāllŏŏ*), or, when they cannot procure this, the swallow-pipe of the *neitiek*. This may be split into threads of different sizes, according to the nature of their work, and is certainly a most admirable material. This, together with any other articles of a similar kind, they p. 173keep in little bags, which are sometimes made of the skin of birds' feet, disposed with the claws downwards in a very neat and tasteful manner. In sewing, the point of the needle is entered and drawn through in a direction towards the body, and not from it or towards one side, as with our sempstresses. They sew the deer-skins with a "round seam," and the water-tight boots and shoes are "stitched." The latter is performed in a very adroit and efficacious manner, by putting the needle only half through the substance of one part of the seal-skin, so as to leave no hole for admitting the water. In cutting out the clothes, the women do it after one regular and uniform pattern, which probably descends unaltered from generation to generation. The skin of the deer's head is always made to form the apex of the hood, while that of the neck and shoulders comes down the back of the jacket; and so of every other part of the animal, which is appropriated to its particular portion of the dress. To soften the seal-skins of which the boots, shoes, and mittens are made, the women chew them for an hour or two together, and the young girls are often seen employed in thus preparing the materials for their mothers. The covering of the canoes is a part of the women's business, in which good workmanship is especially necessary to render the whole smooth and water-tight. The skins, which are those of the *neitiek* only, are prepared by scraping off the hair and the fleshy parts with an *ooloo*, and stretching them out tight on a frame, in which state they are left over the lamps or in the sun for several days to dry; and after this they are well chewed by the women to make them fit for working. The dressing of leather and of skins in the hair is an art which the women have brought to no inconsiderable degree of p. 174perfection. They perform this by first cleansing the skin from as much of the fat and fleshy matter as the *ooloo* will take off, and then rubbing it hard for several hours with a blunt scraper, called *siākŏŏt*, so as nearly to dry it. It is then put into a vessel containing urine, and left to steep a couple of days, after which a drying completes the process. Skins dressed in the hair are, however, not always thus steeped; the women, instead of this, chewing them for hours together, till they are quite soft and clean. Some of the leather thus dressed looked nearly as well as ours, and the hair was as firmly fixed to the pelt; but there was in this respect a very great difference, according to the art or attention of the housewife. Dyeing is an art wholly unknown to them. The women are very expert at platting, which is usually done with three threads of sinew; if greater strength is required, several of these are twisted slackly together, as in the bowstrings. The quickness with which some of the women plat is really surprising; and it is well that they do so, for the quantity required for the bows alone would otherwise occupy half the year in completing it.

It may be supposed that among so cheerful a people as the Esquimaux there are many games or sports practised; indeed, it was rarely that we visited their habitations without seeing some engaged in them. One of these our gentlemen saw at Winter Island, on an occasion when most of the men were absent from the huts on a sealing excursion, and in this Iligliuk was the chief performer. Being requested to amuse them in this way, she suddenly unbound her hair, platted it, tied both ends together to keep it out of her way, and then, stepping out into the middle of the hut, began to make the most hideous faces that can be conceived, by drawing both p. 175lips into her mouth, poking forward her chin, squinting frightfully, occasionally shutting one eye, and moving her head from side to side as if her neck had been dislocated. This exhibition, which they call *ăyŏkĭt-tāk-poke*, and which is evidently considered an accomplishment that few of them possess in perfection, distorts every feature in the most horrible manner imaginable, and would, I think, put our most skilful horse-collar grinners quite out of countenance.

The next performance consists in looking stedfastly and gravely forward and repeating the words *tăbāk-tabak, kĕibō-keibo, kĕ-bāng-ĕ-nū-tŏ-ĕĕk, kebangenutoeek, ămātămā, amatama*, in the order in which they are here placed, but each at least four times, and always by a peculiar modulation of the voice, speaking them in pairs, as they are coupled above. The sound is made to proceed from the throat in a way much resembling ventriloquism, to which art it is indeed an approach. After the last *amatama* Iligliuk always pointed with her finger towards her body, and pronounced the word *angetkook*, steadily retaining her gravity for five or six seconds, and then bursting into a loud laugh, in which she was joined by all the rest. The women sometimes produce a much more guttural and unnatural sound, repeating principally the word *īkkĕrĕe-ikkeree*, coupling them as before, and staring in such a manner as to make their eyes appear ready to burst out of their sockets with the exertion. Two or more of them will sometimes stand up face to face, and with great quickness and regularity respond to each other, keeping such exact time that the sound appears to come from one throat instead of several. Very few of the females are possessed of this accomplishment, which is called *pitkoo-she-rāk-poke*, and it is not p. 176uncommon to see several of the younger females practising it. A third part of the game, distinguished by the word *keitīk-poke*, consists only in falling on each knee alternately, a piece of agility which they perform with tolerable quickness, considering the bulky and awkward nature of their dress.

The last kind of individual exhibition was still performed by Iligliuk, to whom in this, as in almost every thing else, the other women tacitly acknowledged their inferiority, by quietly giving place to her on every occasion. She now once more came forward, and letting her arms hang down loosely and bending her body very much forward, shook herself with extreme violence, as if her whole frame had been strongly convulsed, uttering at the same time, in a wild tone of voice, some of the unnatural sounds before mentioned.

This being at an end, a new exhibition was commenced, in which ten or twelve women took a part, and which our gentlemen compared to blind man's buff. A circle being formed, and a boy despatched to look out at the door of the hut, Iligliuk, still the principal actress, placed herself in the centre, and after making a variety of guttural noises for about half a minute, shut her eyes, and ran about till she had taken hold of one of the others, whose business it then became to take her station in the centre, so that almost every woman in her turn occupied this post, and in her own peculiar way, either by distortion of countenance or other gestures, performed her part in the game. This continued three-quarters of an hour, and, from the precaution of placing a look-out, who was withdrawn when it was over, as well as from some very expressive signs which need not here be mentioned, there is reason to believe that it is usually p. 177followed by certain indecencies, with which their husbands are not to be acquainted. Kaoongut was present indeed on this occasion, but his age seemed to render him a privileged person; besides which his own wife did not join in the game.

The most common amusement, however, and to which their husbands made no objection, they performed at Winter Island expressly for our gratification. The females, being collected to the number of ten or twelve, stood in as large a circle as the hut would admit, with Okotook in the centre. He began by a sort of half-howling, half-singing noise, which appeared as if designed to call the attention of the women, the latter soon commencing the *Amna Aya* song hereafter described. This they continued without variety, remaining quite still while Okotook walked round within the circle; his body was rather bent forward, his eyes sometimes closed, his arms constantly moving up and down, and now and then hoarsely vociferating a word or two, as if to increase the animation of the singers, who, whenever he did this, quitted the chorus and rose into the words of the song. At the end of ten minutes they all left off at once, and, after one minute's interval commenced a second act precisely similar and of equal duration, Okotook continuing to invoke their Muse as before. A third act which followed this varied only in his frequently towards the close throwing his feet up before and clapping his hands together, by which exertion he was thrown into a violent perspiration. He then retired, desiring a young man (who, as we were informed, was the only individual of several then present thus qualified) to take his place in the centre as master of the ceremonies, when the same antics as before were again gone through. After this p. 178description it will scarcely be necessary to remark that nothing can be poorer in its way than this tedious singing recreation, which, as well as everything in which dancing is concerned, they express by the word *mŏmēk-poke*. They seem, however, to take great delight in it; and even a number of the men, as well as all the children, crept into the hut by degrees to peep at the performance.

The Esquimaux women and children often amuse themselves with a game not unlike our "skip-rope." This is performed by two women holding the ends of a line and whirling it regularly round and round, while a third jumps over it in the middle according to the following order:—She commences by jumping twice on both feet, then alternately with the right and left, and next four times with the feet slipped one behind the other, the rope passing once round at each jump. After this she performs a circle on the ground, jumping about half-a-dozen times in the course of it, which bringing her to her original position, the same thing is repeated as often as it can be done without entangling the line. One or two of the women performed this with considerable agility and adroitness, considering the clumsiness of their boots and jackets, and seemed to pride themselves in some degree on the qualification. A second kind of this game consists in two women holding a long rope by its ends and whirling it round in such a manner, over the heads of two others standing close together near the middle of the bight, that each of these shall jump over it alternately. The art therefore, which is indeed considerable, depends more on those whirling the rope than on the jumpers, who are, however, obliged to keep exact time, in order to be ready for the rope passing under their feet.

The whole of these people, but especially the women, p. 179are fond of music, both vocal and instrumental. Some of them might be said to be passionately so, removing their hair from off their ears and bending their heads forward, as if to catch the sounds more distinctly, whenever we amused them in this manner. Their own music is entirely vocal, unless indeed the drum or tambourine before mentioned be considered an exception.

The voices of the women are soft and feminine, and when singing with the men are pitched an octave higher than theirs. They have most of them so far good ears that, in whatever key a song is commenced by one of them, the rest will always join in perfect unison. After singing for ten minutes, the key had usually fallen a full semitone. Only two of them, of whom Iligliuk was one, could catch the tune as pitched by an instrument; which made it difficult with most of them to complete the writing of the notes, for if they once left off they were sure to re-commence in some other key, though a flute or violin were playing at the time.

During the season passed at Winter Island, which appears to have been a healthy one to the Esquimaux, we had little opportunity of becoming acquainted with the diseases to which they are subject. Our subsequent intercourse with a greater number of these people at Igloolik having unfortunately afforded more frequent and fatal instances of sickness among them, I here insert Mr. Edwards's remarks on this subject: —

"Exempted as these people are from a host of diseases usually ascribed to the vitiated habits of more civilised life, as well as from those equally numerous and more destructive ones engendered by the pestilential effluvia that float in the atmosphere of more favoured climes, the diversity of their maladies is, as might `priori be p. 180inferred, very limited. But, unfortunately, that improvidence which is so remarkable in their kindred tribes is also with them proof against the repeated lessons of bitter experience they are doomed to endure. Alternate excesses and privations mark their progress through life, and consequent misery in one or another shape is an active agent in effecting as much mischief amongst them as the diseases above alluded to produce in other countries. The mortality arising from a few diseases and wretchedness combined, seems sufficient to check anything like a progressive increase of their numbers. The great proportion of deaths to births that occurred during the period of our intercourse with them has already been noticed.

"It is doubtful in what proportion the mortality is directly occasioned by disease. Few perhaps die, in the strict sense of the term, a natural death. A married person of either sex rarely dies without leaving destitute a parent, a widow, or a helpless female infant. To be deprived of near relations is to be deprived of everything; such unfortunates are usually abandoned to their fate, and too generally perish. A widow and two or three children left under these circumstances were known to have died of inanition, from the neglect and apathy of their neighbours, who jeered at the commanders of our ships on the failure of their humane endeavours to save what the Esquimaux considered as worthless.

"Our first communication with these people at Winter Island gave us a more favourable impression of their general health than subsequent experience confirmed. There, however, they were not free from sickness. A catarrhal affection in the month of February became generally prevalent, from which they readily recovered after the exciting causes—intemperance and exposure to p. 181wet—had ceased to operate. A solitary instance of pleurisy also occurred, which probably might have ended fatally but for timely assistance. Our intercourse with them in the summer was more interrupted; but at our occasional meetings they were observed to be enjoying excellent health. It is probable that their certain supplies of food, and the nomad kind of life they lead in its pursuit during that season, are favourable to health. Nutrition goes on actively, and an astonishing increase of strength and fulness is acquired. Active diseases might now be looked for, but that the powers of nature are providentially exerted with effect.

"The unlimited use of stimulating animal food, on which they are from infancy fed, induces at an early age a highly plethoric state of the vascular system. The weaker over-distended vessels of the nose quickly yield to the increased impetus of the blood, and an active hemorrhage relieves the subject. As the same causes continue to be applied in excess at frequent intervals, and are followed by similar effects, a kind of vicarious hemorrhage at length becomes established by habit; superseding the intervention of art, and having no small share in maintaining a balance in the circulating system. The phenomenon is too constant to have escaped the observation of those who have visited the different Esquimaux people; a party of them has indeed rarely been seen that did not exhibit two or three instances of the fact.

"About the month of September the approach of winter induced the Esquimaux at Igloolik to abandon their tents and to retire into their more established village. The majority were here crowded into huts of a permanent construction, the materials composing the sides being stones and the bones of whales, and the roofs being formed p. 182of skins, turf, and snow; the rest of the people were lodged in snow-huts. For a while they continued very healthy; in fact, as long as the temperature of the interior did not exceed the freezing-point, the vapours of the atmosphere congealed upon the walls, and the air remained dry and tolerably pure; besides, their hard-frozen winter stock of walrus did not at this time tempt them to indulge their appetites immoderately. In January the temperature suffered an unseasonable rise, some successful captures of walrus also took place, and these circumstances, combined perhaps with some superstitious customs, of which we were ignorant, seemed the signal for giving way to sensuality. The lamps were accumulated and the kettles more frequently replenished, and gluttony in its most disgusting form became for a while the order of the day. The Esquimaux were now seen wallowing in filth, while some surfeited lay stretched upon their skins enormously distended, and with their friends employed in rolling them about to assist the operations of oppressed nature. The roofs of their huts were no longer congealed, but dripping with wet and threatening speedy dissolution. The air was in the bone-huts damp, hot, and, beyond sufferance, offensive with putrid exhalations from the decomposing relics of offals, or other animal matter, permitted to remain from year to year undisturbed in these horrible sinks.

"What the consequences might have been had this state of affairs long continued, it is not difficult to imagine; but, fortunately for them, an early and gradual dispersion took place, so that by the end of January few individuals were left in the village. The rest, in divided bodies, established themselves in snow-huts upon the sea-ice at some distance from the land. Before this change had p. 183been completed, disorders of an inflammatory character had appeared. A few went away sick, some were unable to remove, and others taken ill upon the ice, and we heard of the death of several about this period.

"The cold snow-huts into which they had moved, though infinitely preferable to those abandoned, were ill-suited to the reception of people already sick or predisposed, from the above-named causes, to sickness; many of them were also deficient in clothing to meet the rigorous weather that followed. Nevertheless, after this violent excitement had passed away, a comparatively good condition of health was enjoyed for the remainder of the winter and spring months.

"Their distance from the ships at once precluded any effectual assistance being rendered them at their huts, and their removal on board with safety; the complaints of those who died at the huts, therefore, did not come under observation. It appears, however, to have been acute inflammation of some of the abdominal viscera, very rapid in its career. In the generality the disease assumed a more insidious and sub-acute form, under which the patient lingered for a while, and was then either carried off by a diarrhœa or slowly recovered by the powers of nature. Three or four individuals who, with some risk and trouble, were brought to the ships, we were providentially instrumental in recovering; but two others, almost helpless patients, were so far exhausted before their arrival that the endeavours used were unsuccessful, and death was probably hastened by their removal.

"Abdominal and thoracic inflammations, in fact, seem to be the only active diseases they have to encounter. Where a spontaneous recovery does not take place, these p. 184prove fatal in a short time. The only instance among them of chronic sequels to those complaints occurred in an old man almost in dotage, whose feeble remains of life were wasting away by an ulceration of the lungs.

"No traces of the exanthematous disorders met our observation. A solitary case of epilepsy was seen in a deaf and dumb boy, who eventually died. Chronic rheumatism occurs, but it is rare and not severe. I have some doubt in saying that scurvy exists among them. A disease, however, having a close affinity to it was witnessed, but as in the only case that came fairly under our notice it was complicated with the symptoms of a previous debilitating disease, the diagnosis was difficult. During the patient's recovery from one of the abdominal attacks above mentioned, the gums were observed to be spongy, separated from the teeth and reverted, bleeding, and in various parts presenting the livid appearance of scorbutic gums. At the same period arose pains of an anomalous description, and of considerable severity about the shoulders and thorax. These gradually yielded as he recovered strength, but were succeeded by other pains and tenderness of the bones and muscles of the thighs and legs. The citric acid was given to him freely from the beginning, until it interfered with his appetite and bowels, when it was omitted. Topical applications were at the same time used, and afterwards continued. Signs of amendment appeared before it became necessary to withhold the vegetable acid, and it was not recurred to while he remained on board. Urged by impatience of control, he left us to join his countrymen before he had well regained his strength; but we saw him on board several times afterwards in a progressive state of improvement, and, though yet weak, free from scorbutic symptoms. p. 185Another instance offered in a woman, whom I saw but once. Her gums were spongy and reverted, but not discoloured; her countenance sallow, lips pale, and she suffered under general debility, without local pain or rigidity of the limbs. She remained in this state for a long time, and eventually, as the weather improved, recovered without assistance.

"That affection of the eyes known by the name of snow-blindness, is extremely frequent among these people. With them it scarcely ever goes beyond painful irritation, whilst among strangers inflammation is sometimes the consequence. I have not seen them use any other remedy besides the exclusion of light; but as a preventive a wooden eye-screen is worn, very simple in its construction, consisting of a curved piece of wood six or seven inches long and ten or twelve lines broad. It is tied over the eyes like a pair of spectacles, being adapted to the forehead and nose, and hollowed out to favour the motion of the eyelids. A few rays of light only are admitted through a narrow slit an inch long, cut opposite to each eye. This contrivance is more simple and quite as efficient as the more heavy one possessed by some who have been fortunate enough to acquire wood for the purpose. This is merely the former instrument complicated by the addition of a horizontal plate projecting three or four inches from its upper rim, like the peak of a jockey's cap. In Hudson's Strait the latter is common, and the former in Greenland, where also we are told they wear with advantage the simple horizontal peak alone.

"There are upon the whole no people more destitute of curative means than these. With the exception of the p. 186hemorrhage already mentioned, which they duly appreciate, and have been observed to excite artificially to cure head-ache, they are ignorant of any rational method of procuring relief. It has not been ascertained that they use a single herb medicinally. As prophylactics they wear amulets, which are usually the teeth, bones, or hair of some animal, the more rare apparently the more valuable. In absolute sickness they depend entirely upon their Angekoks, who, they persuade themselves, have influence over some submarine deities who govern their destiny. The mummeries of these impostors, consisting in pretended consultations with their oracles, are looked upon with confidence, and their mandates, however absurd, superstitiously submitted to. These are constituted of unmeaning ceremonies and prohibitions generally affecting the diet, both in kind and mode, but never in quantity. Seal's flesh is forbidden, for instance, in one disease, that of the walrus in the other; the heart is denied to some and the liver to others. A poor woman, on discovering that the meat she had in her mouth was a piece of fried heart instead of the liver, appeared horrorstruck; and a man was in equal tribulation at having eaten, by mistake, a piece of meat cooked in his wife's kettle.

"This charlatanerie, although we may ridicule the imposition, is not, however, with them, as it is with us, a positive evil. In the total absence of the medical art, it proves generally innoxious; while in many instances it must be a source of real benefit and comfort, by buoying up the sick spirit with confident hopes of recovery, and eventually enabling the vital powers to rise superior to the malady, when, without such support, the sufferer p. 187might have sunk under its weight. It was attempted to ascertain whether climate effected any difference in animal heat between them and ourselves by frequently marking the temperature of the mouth; but the experiments were necessarily made, as occasion offered, under such various states of vascular excitement, as to afford nothing conclusive. As it was, their temperature varied from 970 to 1020, coinciding pretty nearly with our own under similar circumstances. The pulse offered nothing singular.

"I may here remark that there is in many individuals a peculiarity about the eye, amounting in some instances to deformity, which I have not noticed elsewhere. It consists in the inner corner of the eye being entirely covered by a duplication of the adjacent loose skin of the eyelids and nose. This fold is lightly stretched over the edges of the eyelids, and forms, as it were, a third palpebra of a crescentic shape. The aperture is in consequence rendered somewhat pyriform, the inner curvature being very obtuse, and in some individuals distorted by an angle formed where the fold crosses the border of the lower palpebra. This singularity depends upon the variable form of the orbit during immature age, and is very remarkable in childhood, less so towards adult age, and then, it would seem, frequently disappearing altogether; for the proportion in which it exists among grown-up persons bears but a small comparison with that observed among the young.

"Personal deformity from mal-conformation is uncommon, the only instance I remember being that of a young woman, whose utterance was unintelligibly nasal, in consequence of an imperfect development of p. 188the palatine bones leaving a gap in the roof of the mouth."

The imperfect arithmetic of these people, which resolves every number above ten into one comprehensive word, prevented our obtaining any very certain information respecting the population of this part of North America and its adjacent islands. The principal stations of these people not visited by us are *Akkoolee, Toonooneeroochiuh, Peelig,* and *Toonoonek,* of whose situation I have already spoken. The first of these, which is the only one situated on the continent, lies in an indentation of considerable depth on the shores of the Polar Sea, running in towards Repulse Bay on the opposite coast, and forming with it the large peninsula situated like a bastion at the north-east angle of America, which I have named Melville Peninsula, in honour of Viscount Melville, the First Lord Commissioner of the Admiralty. From what we know of the habits and disposition of the Esquimaux, which incline them always to associate in considerable numbers, we cannot well assign a smaller population than fifty souls to each of the four principal stations abovementioned; and including these, and the inhabitants of several minor ones that were occasionally named to us, there may perhaps be three or four hundred people belonging to this tribe with whom we have never had communication. In all their charts of this neighbourhood they also delineate a tract of land to the eastward, and somewhat to the northward, of Igloolik, where they say the *Seadlērmeoo*, or strangers, live, with whom, as with the Esquimaux of Southampton Island, and all others coming under the same denomination, they have seldom or never any intercourse, either of a friendly or a hostile p. 189nature. It is more than probable that the natives of the inlet called the river Clyde, on the western coast of Baffin's Bay, are a part of the people thus designated; and, indeed, the whole of the numerous bays and inlets on that extensive and productive line of coast may be the residence of great numbers of Esquimaux, of whom these people possess no accurate information.

Whatever may be the abundance sometimes enjoyed by these people, and whatever the maladies occasioned by their too frequent abuse of it, it is certain that they occasionally suffer very severely from the opposite extreme. A remarkably intelligent woman informed Captain Lyon that two years ago some Esquimaux arrived at Igloolik from a place near Akkoolee, bringing information that during a very grievous famine one party of men had fallen upon another and killed them; and that they afterwards subsisted on their flesh while in a frozen state, but never cooked nor even thawed it. This horrible account was soon after confirmed by Toolemak on board the *Fury*; and though he was evidently uneasy at our having heard the story, and conversed upon it with reluctance, yet by means of our questions he was brought to name, upon his fingers, five individuals who had been killed on this occasion. Of the fact therefore there can be no doubt; but it is certain, also, that we ourselves scarcely regarded it with greater horror than those who related it; and the occurrence may be considered similar to those dreadful instances on record, even among civilised nations, of men devouring one another, in wrecks or boats, when rendered desperate by the sufferings of actual starvation.

The ceremony of crying, which has before been p. 190mentioned as practised after a person's death, is not, however, altogether confined to those melancholy occasions, but is occasionally adopted in cases of illness, and that of no very dangerous kind. The father of a sick person enters the apartment, and after looking at him for a few seconds without speaking, announces by a kind of low sob his preparation for the coming ceremony. At this signal every other individual present composes his features for crying, and the leader of the chorus then setting up a loud and piteous howl, which lasts about a minute, is joined by all the rest, who shed abundant tears during the process. So decidedly is this a matter of form, unaccompanied by any feeling of sorrow, that those who are not relatives shed just as many tears as those that are; to which may be added that in the instances which we witnessed there was no real occasion for crying at all. It must therefore be considered in the light of a ceremony of condolence, which it would be either indecorous or unlucky to omit.

I have already given several instances of the little care these people take in the interment of their dead, especially in the winter season; it is certain, however, that this arises from some superstitious notion, and particularly from the belief that any heavy weight upon the corpse would have an injurious effect upon the deceased in a future state of existence; for even in the summer, when it would be an easy matter to secure a body from the depredations of wild animals, the mode of burial is not essentially different. The corpse of a child observed by Lieutenant Palmer, he describes "as being laid in a regular but shallow grave, with its head to the north-east. It was decently dressed in a good deer-skin jacket, p. 191and a seal-skin, prepared without the hair, was carefully placed as a cover to the whole figure, and tucked in on all sides. The body was covered with flat pieces of limestone, which, however, were so light that a fox might easily have removed them. Near the grave were four little separate piles of stones, not more than a foot in height, in one of which we noticed a piece of red cloth and a black silk handkerchief, in a second a pair of child's boots and mittens, and in each of the others a whalebone pot. The face of the child looked unusually clean and fresh, and a few days only could have elapsed since its decease."

These Esquimaux do not appear to have any idea of the existence of One Supreme Being, nor indeed can they be said to entertain any notions on this subject, which may be dignified with the name of Religion. Their superstitions, which are numerous, have all some reference to the preternatural agency of a number of *toŏrngŏw*, or spirits, with whom, on certain occasions, the Angetkooks pretend to hold mysterious intercourse, and who in various and distinct ways are supposed to preside over the destinies of the Esquimaux. On particular occasions of sickness or want of food the Angetkooks contrive, by means of a darkened hut, a peculiar modulation of the voice, and the uttering of a variety of unintelligible sounds, to persuade their countrymen that they are descending to the lower regions for this purpose, where they force the spirits to communicate the desired information. The superstitious reverence in which these wizards are held, and a considerable degree of ingenuity in their mode of performing their mummery, prevent the detection of the imposture, and secure implicit confidence in these absurd oracles. My p. 192friend Captain Lyon having particularly directed his attention to this part of their history during the whole of our intercourse with these people, and intending to publish his Journal, which contains much interesting information of this nature, I shall not here enter more at large on the subject. Some account of their ideas respecting death, and of their belief in a future state of existence, have already been introduced in the course of the foregoing pages, in the order of those occurrences which furnished us with opportunities of observing them.